FALL

TO

GRACE

THE CLIMB, COLLAPSE, AND COMEBACK OF COACH DAVE BLISS

DAVE BLISS

WITH STEPHEN COPELAND
FOREWORD BY KEN BLANCHARD

FALL TO GRACE

visit the website at **www.daveblissbook.com**

Published by The Core Media Group, Inc., P.O. Box 2037, Indian Trail, NC 28079.

Cover & Interior Design: Nadia Guy
Back Cover Image: Memoir Photography

Printed in the United States of America.

CONTENTS

Contents

FOREWORD

by Ken Blanchard

I have known Dave Bliss since we were in school together at Cornell, where he was an all-Ivy League basketball player. Over the years I've followed his success as a coach. When his demise occurred at Baylor, I tried to get hold of him but he was incognito.

I was thrilled, therefore, when Dave resurfaced, and I have been excited about his journey from the depths as he has grown in his relationship with the Lord. He had always been a Sunday Christian, but he never knew really in his heart what grace was all about—that God loves us no matter what and is always there to pick us up when we are down to help guide our lives back in the right direction.

What happened to Dave happens to a lot of people who experience success. Our ego gets in the way, and we think life is all about us and our wins and accomplishments. In this case, E.G.O. stands for Edging God Out.

In *Fall to Grace*, you will follow Dave's E.G.O. journey. At first, you see him filled with false pride—having a "more than" attitude about life, ultimately thinking he was above it all, including the rules and regulations. The result was his downfall at Baylor, as you see his ego now move to fear and self-doubt—having a "less than" attitude, eventually thinking he was not as good as others, continually beating himself up over what he did, as he focused his energy on protecting himself.

As you read this wonderful book, you'll learn—as Dave did—that the antidote for false pride is humility and the antidote for fear and self-doubt is trusting the unconditional love of God.

Sorry, Dave, that you had to go through such a tough time, but I praise you for sharing your vulnerability and helping all of us realize the power of grace. What an amazing story.

This is a book I recommend to all who want to take their faith to a whole different level and really bring Jesus into their life on a day-to-day basis. As you read *Fall to Grace* and see the changes Dave went through, it might be helpful for you to reflect and look at your life. Oswald Chambers said it well in his book *My Utmost for His Highest*: "The majority of us cannot hear anything but ourselves. And we cannot hear anything God says. But to be brought to the place where we can hear the call of God is to be profoundly changed."

I encourage you to read this book—it could really make a significant difference in your life.

Ken Blanchard is a New York Times *bestselling author who has co-authored over 30 bestselling books including* The One Minute Manager *and* Lead Like Jesus

A NOTE TO THE READER

by Dave Bliss

Some of you are familiar with my story, but in a nutshell, after coaching thirty-six years at the Division I level, I committed several NCAA violations between 2002 and 2003, including personally paying the scholarships of two players. When an unrelated murder occurred involving one of the players, I panicked, was caught on tape attempting a cover-up of the payments, and an unbelievable set of circumstances resulted in my resignation. You could say that my life spiraled out of control.

All that said, this book is not meant to be a denial or an attempt at explaining away my bizarre actions in 2003. I am not a preacher, but I do have a story about God's undeserved grace and forgiveness that I have experienced and how it is available to all that come humbly before His throne. I don't think for a minute any of you would do something as foolish as what I did, but you need to understand something: I didn't think I would, either.

What I discovered was that my spiritual journey in my ten years following the scandal was far more meaningful than my worldly journey in my sixty years prior. Though I had spent most of my life unaware and ignorant of God's love for me, I awakened to my true identity, ironically, after my world fell to pieces.

Woven into the narrative of this book are details taken from ten years of journal entries and another one hundred-plus pages of personal reflections. Because my sins seemed to cast me off on an island, all I did was read and write and then read and write some more. I read Charles Stanley, C.S. Lewis, Rick Warren, Chuck Swindoll, A.W. Tozer, Brennan Manning, and many others. In a broken and surrendered state, I was obsessed with this idea of God-discovery. I read through the entire Bible and then I read it again; I also read Warren's *The Purpose Driven Life* over and over; and as my hope was restored, my life took on a new purpose.

Even today, as I wrestle with the decisions I've made, I am reminded of a quote from Chapter 39 of *The Purpose Driven Life*: "You owe it to future generations to preserve the testimony of how God helped you fulfill His purposes on earth."

With Rick Warren's thought in mind, my obedience to what God can do with my story is truly what drives me nowadays. Although there are parts of my story that I certainly am not proud of, I am grateful for God's faithfulness.

Here is my story.

I always called myself a Christian; I just never knew how much God loved me, which has made me wonder: Was I ever a Christian at all?

PART 1

BLINDED

.

01

BALLOON

I stood behind the podium in disbelief.

It was August 2003, and there were TV cameramen everywhere, all thrusting a microphone in my face and shouting out questions regarding the developing scandal within the basketball program at Baylor University in Waco, Texas. ESPN was there, CNN, FOX, as well as writers from Dallas and Houston.

As the sea of media looked up at me with curious eyes, I, for the first time in four years, struggled with what I should say to them. Even after a tough loss, I would answer their questions respectfully. But now, in this shattered moment, I was an empty shell, in complete shock of what was occurring. My life was unraveling so rapidly that I could not react to the enormity of the gathering storm.

As I finished the short statement announcing my resignation as head men's basketball coach at Baylor University, I couldn't help but reflect back four years earlier when I had been introduced amid cheering and back-slapping as the Bears' next basketball coach. People envisioned me to be the savior of Baylor men's basketball, but now, as I walked to my car outside the administration building, I was alone and the Baylor faithful were in shock—and they weren't the only ones. As I drove home to tell my wife, Claudia, what had just transpired, I knew I would have to explain away the series of lies I had been telling her.

As bad as everything seemed, it was all going to get worse.

Everything I had built, everything I knew to be true, suddenly exploded like a popped balloon.

02

STRAIGHTJACKET SANTA CLAUS

My childhood featured an event that, had it ended differently, would have made this book impossible. Because I was three or four, I relied on others to tell me about it.

Apparently, it all happened one winter mid-day when my dad was home for lunch. He had gone upstairs to check on me while I was napping, but when he walked into my bedroom, I was nowhere to be found. There was, however, an open window and a path through some snow on the roof outside the third-story window. Our house was situated on a sloped hill so that, although the front of our house had two stories, the back of our house had three.

No sooner had Dad gone upstairs than he was running back down the stairs full speed past my mom. As my dad was sprinting out the front door and around the house to look for me, I was walking up the driveway, crying and holding a toy car that had apparently taken the "trip" with me. The guess was that I opened the window, ventured out a little too far, and had slid down from the third story, landing in a four-prong clothesline below.

That theory developed because the clothesline was a little bent, some of the ropes were askew, but there was not a single scratch on me. To this day, I am not fond of heights or roller coasters.

~⁊

My earliest memories in life are being around a lot of people and really enjoying it. I was a "boy sandwich"—three older sisters

(Ann, Nancy, Sally) and one younger sister (Virginia), in a house with my mom (Janice) and dad (Paul). Two of the girls, Ann and Sally, were actually my cousins whose parents (my aunt and uncle) died in a plane crash when I was very young. For all intents and purposes, I remember them as my sisters.

Growing up, I don't remember being without too much, but I know we certainly weren't rich. I had a couple of shirts, a pair of dungarees, a pair of dress gabardines, some sweaters, and a couple of coats. We lived in a typical neighborhood in upstate New York in a town called Binghamton. Located at the confluence of two rivers—the Susquehanna and the Chenango—Binghamton was nicknamed the "Parlor City" because, for the most part, the city had a neat appearance.

The town's population had doubled in size since the early 1900s with the influx of many immigrants. Poles, Irishmen, Italians, Slovaks, and Germans had matriculated from Ellis Island in New York City to Binghamton, hoping to find a job in the area's primary industry: making shoes.

My father worked for a company called Agfa-Ansco, which predated Kodak in the photography business. Years later he became a commercial artist for a local utility company. My mother was a homemaker—pretty basic stuff right out of *Leave It to Beaver*.

Although I grew up in the north where it was cold five months of the year, I really enjoyed being outside. There weren't many fences between neighbors, just trees and hedges, so you could run all over the place. I knew every hiding place within a half-mile of our house. I knew escape routes, cracked sidewalks, and all the good climbing trees. I knew where the asparagus was planted two houses down, where the great-smelling mint grew one street over, and where the best lilac bushes on the block were for hide-and-seek.

The other neighborhood boys and I would run around acting like we were Roy Rogers, Hopalong Cassidy, or Gene Autry—cowboy heroes of the day. I loved watching the black-and-white westerns on Saturday afternoons down at the Jarvis Theatre on Main Street.

From the "cowboy stage," I moved on to enjoy sports, especially baseball. This passion for sports continued as I went through elementary school and junior high. And by the time I got to Binghamton Central High School—a terrific school that *The Twilight Zone* creator Rod Serling had attended—I was playing baseball, basketball, and football.

My next stage of life, college, had a curious beginning.

During my senior year in high school, I had been named to the All-Conference basketball team, and the local newspaper sponsored a dinner at the Elks Hall in Binghamton. All the honorees and their parents were invited to the dinner where Sam MacNeil, the basketball coach at Cornell, was the guest speaker.

Later that evening, after Coach MacNeil had spoken, we were passing in the hall. He stopped me and asked if I had decided where I wanted to go to college. Not everyone went to college in those days, but I had thought about it a little and actually had visited Colgate, Hobart, and a few small schools in the area. But when he asked if I might be interested in visiting Cornell, I was immediately interested. My parents were thrilled that I had a chance to visit a school as prestigious as Cornell and took me up to Ithaca the following Saturday.

On the visit, Coach MacNeil challenged me to a game of handball. (You couldn't do this nowadays because it would be construed as a tryout.) I think he was trying to find out how competitive I was. I must have passed the test because a week later he invited me to become a member of the Big Red. I accepted immediately.

Was connecting with Coach MacNeil a coincidence?

Is there such a thing as coincidences?

In the fall of 1961, I entered Cornell as a two-sport athlete (baseball and basketball), and for the first couple of months I was typically homesick. Cornell was about an hour from Binghamton, so if I wanted to go home, I usually hitchhiked.

The academics at Cornell were a great deal more difficult than I was used to, and I struggled at first. This struggle, however, taught me how important it was to manage my time and place academics before athletics. Once in my first year at Cornell, my freshman coach, Charlie McCord, didn't let me travel to my hometown to play against the local junior college, Broome Tech, because I had done poorly on a chemistry test. I was both heartbroken and embarrassed, but I never let it happen again. In fact, it was the only basketball game I missed over the next four years.

My senior year was a breakout season for Cornell basketball and for me. I was the starting off-guard, whose primary duties were to play defense against the opponent's best player, get some steals and rebounds, and hit an occasional open jump shot. We lost early-season games to Colorado State and UConn, but had a couple of great wins against Syracuse University. The 1964-65 Orange were outstanding, featuring Dave Bing (future Hall of Famer and Detroit Piston) and Jim Boeheim (future Hall of Fame Syracuse coach), but we were really hitting on all cylinders, and this made us pretty confident going into the Ivy League season. We won our first three Ivy League games and stood 11-2 as we prepared for a game against the best team in our conference: Princeton.

This nationally-ranked Princeton team had its two-time All-American Bill Bradley and had won the Ivy League title the previous two seasons. They were picked to repeat. Both teams were undefeated in league play heading into the game.

Several days before the game, Coach MacNeil called me into his office and directed me to sit down in the chair in front of his gray, metal desk. He fumbled with a few notes and then stopped and looked directly at me with his steel-blue eyes. As he squinted at me, he quietly said, "One of us in this room is going to have a chance to guard Bill Bradley this Saturday." I don't think he thought for one minute that I could stop him. Beyond Bradley's remarkable ability, he was also seven inches taller than me. But Coach *did* think I could "harass" him and block him out. Nowadays this basketball strategy might have been called a Box-and-One Defense—my teammates playing their men loosely with me chasing Bradley.

Chasing, I could do. Amazingly enough, this plan worked—at

least for the first twenty minutes. Bradley only scored 6 points in the first half, and we had a 10-point lead. The entire atmosphere at Barton Hall, where Cornell played its home games, was electric. Normally 2,500 to 3,000 people attended the games, but the crowd swelled past 9,000 that evening—which was unheard of at the time, and is still a record.

The game changed dramatically in the second half, however, and Bradley ended up with his usual 30 points. As a result, Princeton caught up, but the evening was meant for the Big Red. A last-second shot by our super-sophomore, Blaine Aston, gave Cornellians a memory that is still remembered as one of the school's greatest games, even fifty years later. We were jubilant!

We ran our winning streak to eleven straight (19-2) before losing to the Yale Bulldogs at home near the end of the season. Our final two games were on the road against Pennsylvania and Princeton.

In those days, the NCAA tournament invited only conference winners and wasn't thought to be much better than the National Invitation Tournament (NIT), which was played in Madison Square Garden in New York City. The biggest prize in our mind was beating Princeton and winning the Ivy title. Despite a great send-off by the Cornell students before our road trip, we lost to both Penn and Princeton.

I scored a career-high 28 points on 14-of-17 shooting the last game of my college career against Princeton, but the game was never close. Evidently Princeton was a pretty good team because the Tigers went to the Final Four that year before losing to Cazzie Russell and a super-talented Michigan team. Then in the "third-place" game, Bradley set the Final Four scoring record that still stands with 56 points as Princeton drubbed Wichita State, 118-82. We didn't end up going anywhere, but I was chosen second-team All-Ivy.

Following basketball, I hung up my sneaks and dusted off my glove for my final year of baseball. In those days, Cornell competed in the Eastern Intercollegiate Baseball League (EIBL), which was made up of the eight Ivy League schools along with Army and

Navy. I had a pretty fair season, hitting around .350 and making the All-EIBL team as an outfielder. I took great pride in my defense, and one of my greatest thrills was throwing out base runners. No question about my biggest "kill"—throwing out future Heisman Trophy winner Roger Staubach when we played Navy.

My senior year, I was selected as the Cornell Athlete of the Year, an award that is still given out by *The Cornell Daily Sun*, the student newspaper. I hadn't thought much about the award during the year because I always thought my classmate Bruce Cohen (football and lacrosse) was more deserving, but it was a great honor and my parents enjoyed the banquet.

I thought my future might be on the baseball diamond. The year 1965 was the first year of the Major League Baseball Draft, and I thought I might get drafted because my college baseball coach had a few scouts approach him and ask about me. The draft, however, came and went without any selection—these scouts somehow seemed to see more in guys like Johnny Bench, Nolan Ryan, and Tom Seaver, who were picked in that draft. For the first time in my young life, I had to look for something to do beyond sports.

I decided to attend graduate school and was accepted into Cornell's Johnson School of Business.

Cornell's Business School, because of the academics, was the hardest period of my young life. I wasn't the last person in the class rank, but I was closer to the bottom than the top. The experience I received, however, was invaluable.

In the spring, after my first semester, all the students were offered the opportunity to interview with various companies (Carnation, Procter & Gamble, IBM, etc.) in anticipation of future job opportunities after graduation. I interviewed with several companies, but my interview with Procter & Gamble went particularly well. My interviewer, Chuck Jarvie, had attended Cornell and many years later would become the CEO of some very successful companies such as Seagram's and Dr Pepper. Chuck must have liked me because I was offered the opportunity of a summer internship with P&G, the largest marketing firm in the world.

An apprenticeship in Chicago gave me a taste of what the business world would be like, and I enjoyed my three months on the job. I worked in the Toilet Goods Division; some of my best products were Crest and Gleem toothpaste and Scope mouthwash. My assigned territory was the near north side of Chicago, and a lot of workdays ended with me trying to complete my sales so I could go to Wrigley Field and watch the final innings of a Cubs game. In those days, the Cubs always played in the afternoons, and you could get in free after the seventh inning.

While in Business School, I worked hard at my studies, but I also had several outside jobs to help pay for my tuition. May 1967 eventually arrived and, despite all my struggling, I graduated from Business School.

What would I do next?

Growing up, I would grade myself on how I was doing in the "Three S's": sports, school, and social. Very rarely did I have two of them going well at the same time, much less three. But what I had neglected was the fourth "S": *spiritual.* How could I have neglected the most important "S"?

When it came to beliefs, I never remember a period when I didn't believe that there was a God, but He seemed so far away. My earliest recollections of anything religious primarily involved activities at my Episcopal church, which was immediately across from my high school. Church activities could range from pancake suppers to Confirmation training, from basketball practice to choir, and from Cub Scouts to Sunday school. This helped me develop a generally positive attitude toward God because all these events were fun experiences.

Throughout my six years at Cornell, I went to church every once in a while and had a somewhat erratic prayer life, especially around exam time. I always enjoyed the feeling I got from attending religious functions, ever since I was an altar boy in the Episcopalian church as a kid. My grandmother would sit there in the first pew and be so proud of me. It gave me a good feeling.

All this formality was about as far away from a "personal relationship with Jesus" as you could get. I never recall thinking God might be interested in my everyday activities. Day-to-day involvement seemed to be the responsibility of my parents and teachers. And just exactly who or what was the Holy Ghost?

I tried as hard as I could to do all the right things. I said "grace" before I ate, prayed when I went to bed, and tried to be nice to people. But I never escaped the feeling that God was "way out there," in the distance, watching over all the troubles of the world. The thought that God was concerned about Dave Bliss on a 24/7 basis never occurred to me. He was too busy helping people who *really* needed help. It seemed to me that He *should* focus on those needy people. I was doing all right, just as I was.

I was growing in confidence and, because I was a "good person," I felt I could make my own decisions regarding what was right and wrong. What might not be good for you might be okay for me because I could "handle it." After all, I was a pretty good guy with good morals. As an example of my self-pious spirit, when I would tell a lie, it was a "white lie," not the malicious ones that "real sinners" tell. Besides, although God was going to be real important once I went to heaven, I didn't have to worry about that for a while. I just had to keep doing "what was right."

I had met some people who called themselves Christians who would talk about surrendering their heart. They seemed to be more dedicated or more "Christian" than me, but I had no idea what it meant or how they got that way. Plus, those types of Christians seemed *too* nice; I felt they were going to get eaten up in this world. I thought if I became one of "those Christians," I wouldn't be able to do what I wanted to do; it would restrict me. Plus, I didn't feel like I needed God quite yet—things were already going pretty good.

Looking back, I can see that the God I worshiped was not the biblical God, but rather, something else of my own creation. The

"God" I claimed throughout much of my life is what I call a "Strait-jacket Santa Claus" God.

I say "straitjacket" because I thought Him to be too restrictive of me—you know, arms all wrapped up, "you can't do this, and you don't do that." And I say "Santa Claus" because that's the way I viewed God—impersonal and legalistic, someone who would give you good things if you acted right. And whenever something good happened, everyone would say, "Praise God!"

Ultimately, this led to me compartmentalizing my life. Church was sacred; sports and school were secular. I didn't mind recognizing God's presence on Sunday mornings, but I assumed He was busy the rest of the week. And maybe I was, too. This was a combination of, one, being too ignorant to welcome Him into my daily life and, two, not knowing He *wanted* to be in my daily life. My view of God was so narrow that I did not know how to involve Him in my everyday activities. If I needed to talk to God, then I needed to go to the church. The rest of the week He was busy with some earthquake or disaster, and I was on my own. Comfortably.

There is an expression that goes, "With God there are no coincidences." But at the time, I didn't see anything in my life that would necessarily be credited to God. I didn't see it as Him protecting me when I fell out of the third-story window, or guiding me to the great opportunities at Cornell, or sharpening me as He created me for a purpose beyond Business School and Procter & Gamble. My image of God had Him busy with the "big things," like taking care of the starving kids in Africa or disasters in Haiti, rather than worrying about little ol' me. But that was an error I made in my God-view. I eventually realized that if I didn't believe God was big enough to be that small—to care about little ol' me—then my view of God wasn't big enough. As I look back on my life, I feel my inability to recognize and appreciate God's hand in my life kept me from enjoying the benefits of a growing, Christ-centered relationship.

Because my view of God was so small, I didn't give Him enough credit for anything at all, and this was because I didn't really *know* Him. Although I never doubted His existence and that He was responsible for my creation, I never realized the importance of a relationship with Him through His Son, Jesus Christ. And because I believed that I was a "good person" and knew right from wrong, I never really felt like I *needed* God to survive in this world. My relationship with God could wait for the next world: heaven. I had this one already under control. Overall, I didn't associate God with love. So why would I need Him?

03

GROUND FLOOR

As I made the three-hour journey up Route 17 from West Point back to Ithaca in the spring of 1967, I remember thinking to myself, "That man is one of the most unusual people I've ever met."

Little did I know, as a fuzzy-cheeked twenty-three-year-old kid, that it would be a day that forever changed my life—the day I interviewed for a coaching job at the United States Military Academy (USMA) at West Point with Bob Knight.

Coach Knight was unusual in the sense that, although I could tell how intelligent and perceptive he was, I could also tell he was intensely driven. I had never met someone with that combination of attributes. I was immediately attracted by these characteristics and felt he was someone who could accomplish great things. I didn't know it then, but my life was about to pick up speed.

I had just received my MBA at the Johnson School of Business at Cornell, but because of the United States conflict in Vietnam, the military draft was looming on my horizon. A draft lottery was held on national TV to determine your draft status. Because I was finished with school, I knew I would be a prime candidate very soon.

During Business School at Cornell, however, I had met a fellow student, Barry Elson, who had played basketball at Dartmouth. He told me about a program at West Point that was looking for a candidate to serve as an "enlisted assistant" assigned to Army basketball. If selected, the program would help fulfill my two-year military requirement.

Two years earlier, during my senior year, Cornell had played

Army in basketball and I had, ironically, been the leading scorer in our win in Ithaca. Taylor "Tates" Locke had been the Army coach at that time, and his assistant was a young man by the name of Bobby Knight. As Coach Knight and I talked during our interview, I could tell that he remembered our Cornell team. I was soon to find out that Bob Knight took note of everything and everyone.

Coach Knight called me a couple of days after my interview and said that, if I volunteered for the draft, it looked good for me to be assigned to the Academy. So, I joined and was sent immediately to Fort Dix, New Jersey.

After ten weeks of Basic Training in Fort Dix during the summer of 1967, I reported to West Point and immediately got my marching orders. Assigned to the Quartermaster Corps at West Point, my responsibility was to travel the length and breadth of the U.S. in search of potential recruits for the USMA—for that college athletic institution commonly called Army. That was my role on Coach Knight's staff: recruit, recruit, and recruit some more.

I would leave the banks of the Hudson River on Labor Day, armed with hundreds of names of potential candidates for the Academy that had been obtained by scouring almost every major newspaper in the country. I would take these names and go to an area, let's say Washington, D.C., and on Monday, make numerous phone calls to local high schools to check the grades of the players I had researched from that area. (You could do that then, but you sure couldn't under federal laws now.) Then, for the remainder of the week, I would visit with the qualified students at their schools. This allowed me to "eyeball" the prospects and determine the extent of their interest.

On the weekend I would drive to the next area, let's say North Carolina, and replicate the same process, until I had covered the East Coast as far south as Florida. This would usually take until the end of September, at which time I would move inland and head back north. Each evening I would call Coach Knight and report on my day's activities. After working my way through Tennessee and Ohio, I would eventually arrive back at West Point for the start of practice on October 15.

After a couple of weeks of practice, I would be back out on the recruiting trail again. My next area was the West Coast. I would catch a C-130 transport jet from McGuire Air Force Base in New Jersey to Travis AFB in Sacramento, California, with an intermediate stop in Chanute AFB in Illinois. It was a real adventure, as the C-130 was one of the most versatile airplanes at the time, used for everything from cargo transport, to troop deployment, to medical evacuation. I hardly ever sat in a normal seat on this flight, as the majority of space on the plane was reserved to accommodate several Payne-Whitney jet engines. I nestled into a net hammock along the inside frame of the plane and every three hours someone—never to be confused with the term of the day, stewardess—would throw me a box lunch. I never had a window and all I could ever hear was the roar of the four huge engines.

Fifteen hours later we'd arrive in Sacramento and board a military bus, which would take me one hundred miles into San Francisco to the Presidio military base, located next to the Golden Gate Bridge. They would assign me a late-model Ford Custom that had no air conditioning, no radio, and nothing automatic. From there I would set out driving south and repeat the same recruiting process as before, spending more time in areas that had military influences, like Fresno and San Diego.

I would travel down the entire coast of California, reach San Diego, take a left (head east), and work through Arizona, New Mexico, and on into Texas. I found it interesting that when I got to Dallas, Texas, it was a shorter distance for me to drive directly back to West Point (1,570 miles) than to retrace my trip all the way back to San Francisco and drop the car off (1,700 miles). I was definitely learning the country.

Each evening I would continue to call Coach Knight and give him a progress report. Coach always made me feel good about what I was doing because it was pretty lonely for weeks at a time, but since he had held the same position three years before, he knew how to give me a boost.

I may have gone to Business School at Cornell with dreams of being an executive at a company like Procter & Gamble, but I was finding out that now I had great interest in being a coach. Working under Coach Knight helped me realize that.

Bob Knight is an artist at instilling confidence in people. Because of his well-publicized temper, many never fully appreciate the great leadership qualities that Coach exhibits.

They say one of the greatest things a leader can do for someone under his command is to help him discover and realize his true potential. Coach Knight has always had the ability to do that. Now, if you sell yourself short or underperform, he will be your worst nightmare; but if you have abilities, he gives you enough rope and trust that you will have opportunities you never imagined. I think another one of Coach Knight's protégés, Duke University head coach Mike Krzyzewski, would agree.

Even now, when some of the "Knight Disciples" get together, one of the first recollections is how much faith Coach had in his assistants. He would get you involved in practice, ask you to participate in clinics, let you schedule, and even give you freedom in recruiting. He saw things in me I never saw in myself.

My two years with Coach Knight at West Point had the experience of five. I was on the road recruiting seven months out of the year, while most schools only recruited for two months out of the year. Since the NCAA didn't have a recruiting period at that time, we recruited every time we could. I kidded people that I was the seventh most important person on his three-man staff.

I listened ardently to everything he ever said, and in the many occasions where I would have to drive him somewhere, I was amazed at how well-versed he was in literature. He might be reading two or three books at a time, a Louis L'Amour western or a Sun Yat-sen book on philosophy. We talked about a variety of subjects on those car rides, everything from General George Patton to baseball legend Ted Williams. I not only learned about basketball from Coach Knight, but I also learned about life. He thought deeply, but very logically. He was pragmatic, but sometimes very mischievous. He would predict the future and then change it moments later.

Ultimately, what Coach Knight became to me at West Point was an older brother. I loved spending time with him, and I knew everything he had me do served a purpose. My two years at West Point had set me on a course that would forever change my life.

Once my two-year military commitment at West Point was up, I was fortunate to be immediately hired in June 1969 by Cornell head coach Jerry Lace as the Big Red's head freshman coach and assistant varsity coach. I was returning to my alma mater.

Returning to Cornell allowed me to really immerse myself in this new "coaching profession." As head freshman coach, I could work on developing my own philosophy, and I was finding my two-year experience at West Point very beneficial. What prepared me most for Cornell were all the recruiting connections I made from being on the road seven months out of the year under Coach Knight. No one in the country had the recruiting experience I had at my age.

Coach Knight and I stayed in touch while I was at Cornell, and during my second season as a coach, fate entered in. My last game of the 1971 season was in Hamilton, New York, versus the Colgate freshmen team that we had already defeated several times earlier in the year. The varsity game that night featured Colgate against Bob Knight's Army squad, the same team that I had helped recruit a few years earlier. I was excited to see Coach Knight.

After defeating the Colgate frosh yet another time, our game ended in a skirmish during the closing handshake. One of their players took a swing at one of our players, and pure havoc was the result. By the time that order had been restored, the Army team was taking the floor for their warm-ups.

It was then that I remember walking into the visiting locker room to wish Coach good luck before tip-off. As I entered, he was sitting on a chair, alone in the locker room, preparing for the game. He was always a little edgy before opening tip-off, so I didn't want to stay too long. We talked for a few minutes, and before I left he said, "I may be giving you a call in a couple weeks."

I was caught off guard, but I sheepishly said, "Great, call me any time." And I walked out of the locker room.

A couple weeks later, on a snowy Easter Sunday in upstate New York, my phone rang in my apartment. I picked up the phone and heard his voice on the other end.

"Where are we going?" I asked him.

"Indiana," he answered.

"Great," I said.

When I hung up the phone, all I could think was, "Here we go."

04

ELEVATOR

I was a twenty-seven-year-old bachelor, and all I owned were three things: a color television, a late-model car, and a corn plant. I don't know why I had a corn plant. I suppose I thought it was cool. One of those weird young-adult phases, I guess. Regardless, I threw my television and plant into my olive-drab (military influence?) Pontiac Le Mans coupe, and made the twelve-hour drive from Ithaca, New York, to Bloomington, Indiana.

As much as I liked where I grew up, it felt good to get out of the Northeast. I had spent my entire life there—from growing up in Binghamton, to attending college and playing sports fifty miles away at Cornell, to serving under Coach Knight at West Point, and finally returning to Cornell to coach.

Going to Indiana was exciting. Everything was new. It was Bob Knight's first year; and it was also the Hoosiers' first year in their new arena, Assembly Hall. There are few better places to coach than at a military academy, but as we were in the midst of the Vietnam Conflict, as it was called then, it was also a difficult place to recruit players because the nation was so divided over the war. Now, though it was several years before the movie *Hoosiers*, we were recruiting in an area that worshipped basketball.

One of the other assistants that Coach hired was Bob Weltlich, who later went on to become a head coach at Mississippi, Texas, South Alabama, and Florida International. Bob W. had followed me at Army in the enlisted assistant position, so we were similarly trained. We would become great friends, and several years later were best men in each other's weddings. And since Bob W. and I were both bachelors at Indiana, we didn't have all the time-consuming family requirements that married coaches might have. We were available, literally 24/7, and spent most of the time working on and thinking about Indiana basketball, especially the accumulation of good players.

Bob W.'s major responsibilities entailed the overall recruiting process and much of the scouting of opponents. He was exceptional at both jobs. My responsibilities were to recruit the state of Indiana and then help Coach Knight with practice. Helping him at practice was sort of a promotion from my West Point days.

As an example of how organized we were and how hard we were working, Bob W. would plan a recruiting trip to, let's say, Chicago and its suburbs. Five of us would pile into the car after lunch on Friday and drive the two and a half hours north to Chicago. One by one, we would drop a coach off at a high school gymnasium and then proceed to the next gym and drop another coach off until all five were watching prospective players. At the conclusion of the games, we would retrace our steps and pick all the coaches up again and drive back to Bloomington.

We might not get back until three or four o'clock in the morning, but we had out recruited the competition that night, for sure. I remember asking Coach if he thought everyone else was working as hard as we were.

"Davy, my boy," he said, "if I thought they were, we would be working even harder."

It may have been demanding work, but Bob W. and I loved it. I didn't know it at the time, but from the moment Bob Knight showed up in Bloomington in 1971, we were on course to creating what has been called one of the greatest college basketball teams of all time: the 1976 Indiana Hoosiers.

Indiana University is renowned for its rich basketball history, but it was Bob Knight who rekindled the coals. There hadn't been much excitement the previous fifteen years. IU had won national championships in 1940 and 1953 under head coach Branch Mc-Cracken, but that was a long time before Bob Knight arrived in Bloomington.

The program that we inherited was lethargic, at best. Although they had recruited several Indiana Mr. Basketball award winners, they were barely above the .500 mark in recent years. It was very much a climb, but the building process would be a great learning experience for both Bob W. and me on how to put programs together.

Almost immediately, however, Coach had successfully brought pride and energy back to the Hoosier program. We finished 17-8 in our first year, losing to Princeton in the NIT. Although we signed some solid recruits our first year at Indiana, we added some big-name recruits in our second season. We signed the Player of the Year from two neighboring states—Scott May was Mr. Ohio, and Quinn Buckner was Mr. Illinois—and we brought in a good harvest in Indiana, including a future great player, Bobby Wilkerson. This was perfect since the 1972-73 season was the first year the NCAA allowed freshmen to play.

Coach was a stern taskmaster, to say the least, both to his assistants and his players. There was sort of a good cop/bad cop dynamic he used with the players. You can take a wild guess as to who played the "bad cop" role, but I think Coach always knew we would support him. And we didn't mind it because we were intensely loyal and knew that what Coach was "suggesting" was going to be good for all of us.

Another reason this firm-hand approach worked so well for Coach was because of the character of the players we were accruing. They were physically gifted, academically driven, and they proved capable of being mentally tough. Bob W. and I both felt that the combination of this quality-type of player, combined with the genius of Bob Knight, would soon prove to be unstoppable.

It looked like another NIT post-season in 1973, but at the end of the year, we defeated Purdue in an afternoon home game in front of the best crowd we'd had since we arrived there, and then we listened to the radio that evening as highly-favored Minnesota choked against last-place Northwestern. This all resulted in us becoming the 1973 Big Ten champions. We beat Marquette in the first round of the NCAA tournament in Nashville, Tennessee, and then defeated Kentucky in the second round, thanks to senior Steve Downing's impressive performance.

The Indiana Hoosiers were going to the Final Four—and over 4,000 crazed Indiana fans greeted us when we landed at the airport after defeating Kentucky.

Basketball in Indiana was back.

Our Final Four opponent ended up being none other than the Wizard of Westwood, John Wooden, and his UCLA Bruins. Downing thoroughly outplayed UCLA's Bill Walton but overall the Bruins proved too much for us. UCLA defeated Memphis State to win the national championship. We beat Providence in the consolation game to finish 22-6 on the year.

When we returned to Bloomington, we were greeted again by thousands of fans, and Coach spoke to the crowd. It had been an incredible season. And Coach had given the Hoosier fans their identity back.

When Coach Knight told me in the offseason that Tulane University called, inquiring about me being their next head coach, I was completely caught off guard. I was only twenty-nine years old and, honestly, had never even considered what it would be like to leave Coach and go somewhere on my own.

Coach urged me to interview for the Tulane job because it would be good practice for other opportunities down the road. The interview with Tulane in New Orleans went fine, but a couple of weeks later, they decided to hire Roanoke College's head coach instead. I couldn't stop thinking about our team at Indiana, anyway. I was obsessed with the program we were building in Bloomington.

As hard as we were working at Indiana, it was also a lot of fun. Earlier that season, I remember an Evansville car dealer named Bill Keck allowing Coach to use one of his cars—a green Buick Electra. (This was the earliest I heard of coaches being provided with loaner cars—good advertising for the car dealer and a perk for the coach.) Then, perhaps as a gesture of gratitude for all our hard work the previous year, Coach let Bob W. and I take the car down to Daytona Beach.

We were excited to get some time off, left Bloomington immediately, and drove straight down to Daytona Beach—a thousand miles in fifteen hours. We arrived mid-afternoon and parked the car on the beach, as you can do at Daytona, and went to a nearby beach bar. Bob W. and I had probably been in the bar for a couple of hours—enjoying the break and escaping a bit from the stresses of basketball—when we heard a slow, articulated, warning come over the speakers in the bar.

"There is a green Buick parked out on the beach that is about to go under," said the voice over the loudspeaker. "Again, whoever's green Buick is parked out on the beach, you better get it before it goes under."

Bob W. and I looked at each other. What would two guys from Indiana know about the ocean's tide? Next thing we knew, we were both sprinting out of the bar toward the beach to rescue poor Bill Keck's Buick from the hungry Atlantic Ocean. Can you imagine if we hadn't "rescued" the car? That would have been an interesting phone call!

But that was Indiana University for us assistants. Everywhere we went, everything we did, there was excitement—whether it involved basketball and Bob Knight or just a couple of bachelors out for a "night on the town."

Life couldn't have been better.

Our third season at Indiana was also the year we started recruiting a kid out of French Lick, Indiana, by the name of Larry Bird.

We heard that Larry was having a good senior season, so we sent one of our graduate assistants down to watch him play. He came back and reported, "I think this guy is pretty good."

So we sent our next recruiter down. When he returned, he said the same thing, "I think this guy is pretty good."

So we sent the next one—and got the same report.

It got to the point where I went down. I returned to Bloomington and Coach Knight asked me, "What do you think?"

I said exactly what everyone else was saying. "I think he's pretty good," I told Coach Knight. "And evidently," I continued, "so does Denny Crum (Louisville's head coach), because he's been there three times this week."

Coach Knight is so competitive, that's all he needed to hear. For the rest of the season, Coach watched Larry play. He was determined to beat out Denny Crum.

We were all correct in our assessment, obviously. At the end of the day, Larry Bird ended up being pretty good.

Meanwhile, though, our third season at Indiana was not turning out as well as we hoped.

Similar to the year before, we finished the season at home against Purdue and squeaked out a one-point victory to put us in a tie with Michigan for the Big Ten championship. There would be a one-game playoff against the Wolverines at Illinois to determine the NCAA tournament representative from the Big Ten.

But as good as we were against Purdue, we were awful against Michigan. The loss landed us in the newly conceived CCA (Collegiate Commissioners Association) tournament, a tournament designed to give the conference runners-up a chance to play in a post-season tourney. It disappeared when the NCAA expanded their post-season tournament the following season.

Playing in the CCA tournament in the postseason after advancing to the Final Four the year before was heartbreaking to all of us, especially for Coach Knight. In the championship game of the

CCA tournament, he was ejected nine minutes into the first half, which meant the next coach in line—me—had to take over.

I really think the pressures of the season and the disappointing playoff loss to Michigan had cascaded down on Coach. He was physically and mentally spent.

When he was tossed, instead of having to leave the arena, as they require nowadays, he just went to the top of the Checker Dome in Saint Louis and sat down. I assumed the coaching position on the bench and watched as our team kept increasing the lead.

Meanwhile, Coach utilized Bob W. as a "runner." Coach would tell him a strategy that he wanted relayed down to me, which Bob W. would deliver to me on the bench.

I actually derived a great deal of confidence through the entire experience because not only did we win the game 85-60, but I must have been reading Coach's mind a lot of times since we were usually already implementing the very strategies he sent down.

I looked up to Coach Knight so much that my greatest confidence in coaching came through the realization that maybe I was beginning to think like him.

Larry Bird ended up coming to Indiana, but he left in September before basketball practice even started. At IU, he was homesick and didn't know how to handle an institution that was sixteen times bigger than his hometown. He moved home, enrolled in a junior college, dropped out, and drove a garbage truck for a year before his historic college career at little Indiana State. You may have heard a little more about him in the NBA after that.

As for our 1974-75 team, we added a number of good players that offseason; but "good" players would have to wait their turn because of the quality of talent at the top. Trying to break into a lineup that was later heralded "the greatest college basketball team of all time" was very difficult. Coach was always very guarded about what he said about his team—that's why I was shocked by a conversation he and I had in January 1975. We were 12-0 and were about to play our second conference game of the year against Michigan. We were walking off the floor following the mid-day shoot-around for the Michigan game when Coach looked me square in the eyes and said, "If we win tonight's game, we might win *every* game."

Coach *never* said stuff like that. And the fact that he said it—with all of his calculations and doubts—made me *really* realize how good a team we had. As things turned out, he was exactly right.

We beat Michigan and ran the table the remainder of the regular season.

The real downer, however, was losing our star player, Scott May, to a broken wrist midway through a game at Purdue a few weeks before the end of the season. The players pulled together, and we finished the Big Ten season 18-0. We cruised through the first two rounds of the NCAA tournament, defeating UTEP and Oregon State, before facing Kentucky in the Elite Eight. We had accomplished all this despite Scott's absence.

In the regular season game against Kentucky, a 98-74 blowout win several months earlier, Coach had accidentally hit Kentucky head coach Joe Hall in the back of the head during the post-game handshake. The press made a big thing of it then, but there is no way that he would have done it on purpose. When the teams met again in the NCAA regional finals at Dayton, everyone else was worried about "the slap" controversy while Indiana was hoping to have Scott May ready to play. Turns out, Scott returned. He was never a factor in the game, however, and the Wildcats nipped us at the end, 92-90.

Just like that, our dreams were over. A 31-1 record, unanimous No. 1 ranking, twenty-point average margin of victory, and utter dominance throughout the season still left us empty-handed. There were a lot of despondent players and coaches in the Indiana locker room. And I was one of them. Our dreams of winning a national championship had been shattered. Driving back to Bloomington, all I could think about was how hard we had worked and how unfortunate it was to have it all end like this.

Of course, Indiana went on to finish with a 32-0 record the following year and win the national championship with an identical team. But it turns out I wasn't alongside them when they won the national title.

I had never been the type of coach who was always looking for his "own job." I hadn't really thought about being a head coach until the previous season when Tulane called. Even then, I was perfectly content to keep helping Coach Knight. I honestly believed I could work under him my entire career.

But at the end of the season, Coach Knight told me that there were three schools who had called about talking to me: Jacksonville, Stanford, and Oklahoma.

"What do you think I should do?" I asked him.

"I think you should talk to them," he told me directly.

As a coach, you learn that there is a time to push your assistants out of the nest, and Coach felt like it was the right time to push me out. I was honored that he believed in me enough to let me go.

Coach was really helpful as I went from job interview to job interview, instructing me on how I should conduct myself and what I should be aware of. He also helped me evaluate the strengths and weaknesses in each of the three schools and direct me toward a place that he thought would be best for me.

First, I flew out to Jacksonville and I was impressed, although it certainly was not Indiana. Next, I traveled to Palo Alto, and I thought the campus was beautiful. I remember being ushered into a second-floor conference room where at least twelve to fifteen people were seated around a large conference table. After some idle conversation, an old, wizened, distinguished, professorial-type asked me, "How are you going to beat John Wooden and UCLA?"

"That's a great question," I laughed. "What I hope is that he'll retire."

And he did . . . two months later.

Overall, my trip to Norman, Oklahoma, was my favorite. From the moment I stepped on campus, I knew it fit me better than the two other opportunities.

Honestly, I wasn't sure if I was ready to be a head coach, but I had confidence that I had been prepared by the best: Bob Knight.

On April 15 at 5 p.m., I received a call from University of Oklahoma athletic director Wade Walker.

"Podner, how would ya like to be our next round-ball coach?" he queried in his Mississippi drawl.

It was official. At thirty-one years old, I was the youngest major college head coach in the country.

05

SOONER

As soon as I accepted the University of Oklahoma job, I had to make some quick decisions, and the first one was whom I would hire as my two assistants. Since I hadn't anticipated getting a job at the end of the 1975 season, I really didn't give it a lot of prior thought. However, after discussing it with Coach Knight and Bob W., I took our two part-time assistants from Indiana with me to Oklahoma: Charlie Harrison and Doug Ash.

Charlie was from North Carolina, had attended Guilford College, and talked with a deep Southern drawl. He had a bum left leg from battling polio as a child, which left him no choice but to coach if he wanted to stay connected to basketball. As a sophomore in high school, he was already coaching seventh and eighth graders. Charlie had a great head of shocking red hair, and he once asked Coach Knight what he had to do to become his graduate assistant at Indiana. "Get a haircut," Knight told him. So he got one, and the rest is history. Charlie was a terrific hire because he was great at thinking outside the box. He was also a terrific offensive mind.

Doug was from Shelbyville, Indiana, and played basketball at Hanover College. He was going to graduate school at Indiana when I met him, and was sent to our coaching staff by legendary Hanover College head coach John Collier.

The day of Doug's first practice, he walked into Assembly Hall with a whistle and a coaching pad. Coach never used a whistle, nor did he let his assistants. As Doug walked in, Coach leaned over to me, watching Doug from afar, and murmured, "Tell that

SOB to take his whistle and jam it up his a**."

Doug never brought a whistle to practice again.

I really lucked out in hiring Charlie and Doug. Charlie was with us at Oklahoma for a couple of years before he joined "Tates" Locke in coaching the NBA's Buffalo Braves. Doug stayed with me for the next twenty-eight years. He could have gone on to be a very successful head coach somewhere, but he chose to stay with me.

At one point, I tried to convince him to be Coach Knight's assistant once the job opened up. "If you want to be a head coach," I told him, "go be Coach's assistant for a year and he'll get you a job."

But he never left my side.

Doug and I began a tradition at Oklahoma that we would continue for nearly three decades. We would get up each morning and meet at the office around 7 a.m., then go on a forty-five-minute run together through the Oklahoma hills or the university's golf course. We would get back to the offices and, whereas I would have a bagel and a cup of coffee, Doug would have a Dr Pepper and some monkey cake.

Throughout the morning, Doug would do his work, and I would do mine. Because we were together for so long, he became very adept at scheduling and recruiting. This allowed me to "work the room," that is, do the extra things like participate in university or community affairs that helped our program. It might range from raising money for the university library or leading a United Fund Drive. He would do the bulk of the office work and, although I would formulate most of the basketball stuff, I always would run it by him.

Then, at noon, we would go on another forty-five-minute run and talk about what we did in the morning. We would get back at 1 p.m., eat lunch, then he would come in my office at 2:30, and we would go over what we were going to do at the 3:30 practice. We would have practice from 3:30 to 6:30, go home, and then repeat the same routine the next day . . . and the next season . . . for the next twenty-eight years.

There were a lot of good coaching duos out there—Smith and Guthridge, Boeheim and Fine—and we were together just as long.

In a day and time when very few coaches had best friends, Doug was my best friend. And no one was better respected among his peers than Doug Ash.

Returning Oklahoma basketball to excellence was one challenge. Convincing a football school to get excited about basketball was quite another.

A mutual friend named Rich Clarkson introduced me to Oklahoma's football coach, Barry Switzer. Rich worked for *Sports Illustrated* and is one of the best sports photographers ever. Because of the success of the respective sports, he covered both Indiana basketball and Oklahoma football. When I got the Oklahoma job, I know Rich called Coach Switzer and put in a good word for me because Coach could not have been nicer to me when I arrived.

I liked all the football coaches, and they made me feel welcome from the beginning. His defensive coordinator's wife, Chris Lacewell, sold me my first house—a neat one-level ranch with an atrium in the middle. I took my television and corn plant, bought some furniture, and set up like I was intending to stay for a while. Some of the alums were asking where I had rented. What did they know that I didn't?

Heading into our first season, I remember one of the football coaches joking that the first sell-out in the Sooners' brand-new basketball arena, the Lloyd Noble Center (LNC), would be for wrestling.

I laughed, but I made a mental note for the future.

The wrestling statement wasn't that inaccurate, unfortunately.

After starting the season 3-7, I remember having a televised game against Oral Roberts at the LNC. The game was a real downer, not just because we lost, but also because there were so few fans in attendance that, before the start of the game, all the spectators in the building (maybe 750) were asked to sit behind the team benches so the television shots would look like there were people at the game.

Was this what it was going to be like at a football school?

Once the football season came to an end, we encouraged the administration to give the football team its well-deserved national championship trophy at our next home game against Oklahoma State. They did, and 8,000 fans showed up as we killed the Cowboys, 57-42. Don't tell me kids don't play harder when people are interested in what they're doing.

We followed that victory with another home win against Iowa State, setting up our only other television game of the year, an afternoon encounter against the heralded Kansas Jayhawks in Allen Field House. It would be a game that would change the direction of our season and give our program a terrific boost.

Despite the boisterous Allen Field House—the "waving wheat" cheers and all—Kansas appeared too bored with having to play the 5-13 Sooners. We got off to a rough start, but we hung around most of the second half, until, with four seconds remaining, our freshman from Lima, Ohio—John McCullough—hit two clutch free throws to secure a 64-63 win. Obviously, we were ecstatic over the victory. After only winning three games on the entire season, we had now won three in a row and were starting to see what we were really capable of—right in the heat of the conference season.

After the game, I shook Kansas head coach Ted Owens' hand and did an interview with John Wooden, who had just retired and was providing color commentary on the game. I then ran to the locker room to congratulate our team following the interview, then ran *back* to the press table to have Coach Wooden autograph the game program as a remembrance of the great victory.

When we returned to Norman, I proudly hung the autographed program up on the wall in my spare bedroom.

Over the years, every time I took a new job, I would move the treasured John Wooden autograph to a different wall in a different house. It always took me back to my first season as a head coach.

Even though our final record that season was 9-17 (6-8 in the conference), I was somehow named the Big Eight Coach of the Year. I'm not sure how many times a person has won Coach of the Year in a major conference with a losing record, but I found it encouraging. The COY award also spoke volumes about how well I had been prepared by Coach Knight. Because I had been taught by the best, I knew that if I could just, somehow, apply what he had taught me, we had a chance to be successful. Although the start of the season had been incredibly trying and emotionally exhausting, it was encouraging to our staff and to me personally that our perseverance was paying off. It also allowed us to recruit on an upswing, giving our program some credibility.

I couldn't imagine anything that could be more meaningful than investing in young men, teaching them to strive for excellence, and watching them succeed. Every time I saw the program with Coach Wooden's autograph, it reminded me of everything I felt that first season—I was right where I was supposed to be.

A number of years passed until one day I glanced at the Oklahoma/Kansas game program hanging on my wall. I noticed John Wooden's autograph was no longer visible. Confused, I walked over and stood directly in front of the autograph. I squinted at the program, but it was apparent that the sun had faded the autograph; the signature had completely disappeared.

I shrugged it off at the time, but now, looking back, I understand what it all symbolized. Something that once had been so important in my life had gradually changed. You don't see it happening, but then one day you look up and it's gone.

06

OVERFLOW

We didn't win many games that first season at Oklahoma, so whenever we did, I would sometimes stay out late with the fellow coaches at a restaurant in Norman called Cross Timbers. Heck, we weren't sure when the next victory would come, so we celebrated. I was very different from Coach Knight in that regard. Coach never drank alcohol, so he relaxed with a big bowl of ice cream while he watched film of the night's game. I usually needed a Bloody Mary, not only to calm my nerves, but to also soothe my throat from yelling at everyone. I never enjoyed the feeling that came from drinking, but I usually needed calming down after a tumultuous couple of hours.

Cross Timbers was the place to go in Norman, especially after a victory in football. During those festive occasions, this spacious establishment would be wall-to-wall with patrons, barely able to hear one another because it was so loud, all clamoring to be served by waitresses who were clad in attractive short dresses.

We would also go to Cross Timbers sometimes after a victory in basketball. One evening, after one of our hard-earned victories, our coaching staff was celebrating at Cross Timbers. On this occasion, it was getting late, so there weren't many people still at the restaurant. We quickly ordered our food and beverages before they closed. I'm sure most of the people in there didn't even know we played (much less won) a basketball game that night. Because of the late hour, it quickly became apparent that our night would end early and our celebration would be cut short. But we hadn't won in a while, and I didn't want the evening to end.

The bartender at Cross Timbers was a nice guy who resembled Tom Selleck (Magnum, P.I.), right down to the full, well-trimmed mustache.

"How much would it cost to keep this bar open?" I joked to him. I was too excited to go home.

He graciously said he would allow us to have a private party while he closed the restaurant to everyone else. In order to serve our crew of coaches and friends, he asked a couple of the waitresses to stay around to help serve our party. One waitress in particular caught my eye. She had pretty, blonde, sun-streaked hair and a beautiful smile.

Several weeks later, after the season was over, I was back in Cross Timbers (probably for our next victory) and was sitting at the bar talking to "Magnum" when that same young lady walked by the bar, as she was seating a couple. I smiled at her, and she smiled politely back.

"Hey," I queried to Magnum as she left, "tell me, what is that waitress's name?"

"That's Claudia Fosnes," he told me.

Fosnes, I said to myself.

The name itself was an unusual one, but it sounded vaguely familiar. After a few minutes, it came to me. A couple of years before, I had tried to recruit a player from Colorado by the name of Jeff Fosnes for our Hoosier squad. Coaches always remember the names of good players.

Thinking back, Jeff Fosnes may be one of the greatest athletes I've ever recruited. I made an attempt to recruit him at the same time we recruited Quinn, Scott, and all the rest, but he ended up going to Vanderbilt because he wanted to attend medical school and become a doctor. Digger Phelps (Notre Dame), Norm Stewart (Missouri), and Ted Owens (Kansas) all made home visits, as did John MacLeod from Oklahoma. Jeff was also being recruited at the same time for football as a quarterback by some big-time football schools. To this day, he is recognized as one of the greatest basketball players in Colorado high school and Vanderbilt history. *Surely*, I thought to myself, *this couldn't be the same family.*

"Where is she from?" I asked him.

"Denver, Colorado," he told me.

I bet they are related, I thought to myself.

I finished my drink and headed toward the exit. That's when I ran smack dab into Claudia. I fumbled for something to say and finally blurted, "Hi, my name is Dave Bliss. Are you related to Jeff Fosnes?"

"Yes," she said, "he's my brother."

It turned out that Jeff had been interested in Oklahoma because he liked Coach MacLeod. Jeff and his family, including Claudia, made a campus visit to OU. And although Jeff decided to go to Vanderbilt, Claudia had seen enough and decided to attend Oklahoma.

"I think Jeff is playing up in Tulsa at the Pizza Hut All-Star Game this Saturday, isn't he?" I continued. "Are you gonna go?"

I was planning on driving up and watching the game because two other invitees were two of our Indiana players, Quinn Buckner and Scott May. I hadn't seen them since they won the national championship earlier in the year for Indiana.

"Yes," she told me, "I'm going with a friend."

Nuts, I thought to myself again. *That's her nice way of telling me she has a boyfriend.*

"Well, maybe I'll see you there," I smiled. "It was a nice to meet you."

"Okay, see you there," she said.

When Friday arrived, I decided to take a date along, and we headed to Tulsa. Almost as soon as we entered, I saw Claudia. It turned out she wasn't with another guy; she was with one of her girl friends. Darn!

Throughout the game, I kept an eye on Claudia, and, at one

point, saw her get up and leave the stands. I turned to my date and told her, "I'm going to run to the restroom."

I am sure my date wondered what had happened to me because I was gone for about fifteen minutes, but I knew that I had found someone special.

A week later, I finally got up the nerve to ask Claudia out.

On our first date, we just drove around in my car and talked. We continued to date throughout the spring and, although she went home to Colorado for summer vacation, I was smitten. I had done the "dating thing" at West Point and Indiana, but when someone walks into your life who is the nicest person you've ever met, the fact that I was thirteen years older than she was didn't make any difference. I realized that there was something special about her.

That summer, I visited her a couple times in Colorado and met her family. They were a family of faith—I always wanted to marry a girl of character and strong values—and I got along great with all of them, especially her father. When she returned to Oklahoma in the fall, all bets were off, and I never dated another woman again.

In the late summer before our second year at OU, Barry Switzer called me and asked me to come down to his office. This had never happened before, but when I walked in, he promptly handed me sixteen season tickets for the home games at Owen Field. I could use them however I saw fit; no strings attached. I was quite surprised, but I took it as an indication that he accepted me as part of the OU team. I was unsure if this would ever happen, especially after an incident that took place the previous fall,

During our pre-season practice in October, I received a call from one of Barry's football assistants.

"Would the football team be able to use the Lloyd Noble Center this afternoon for a light practice?" I was asked. It was forecast to be stormy that afternoon, and the Sooner football team wanted to use someplace indoors. I didn't know what to say. As much as I knew football "ruled the athletic roost" at OU, I knew if I gave in it might become a regular occurrence, which I didn't need.

"Boy, I'm not sure," I finally told him. "I think we'll be using it."

After I hung up, I expected to receive a call any minute from our athletic director, Wade Walker, or maybe even the governor of Oklahoma, telling me different. Fortunately, however, the weather changed and it was all forgotten.

Overall, though, it was great to be at OU during this period. Barry couldn't have been nicer if he tried. He was a terrific person and a neat guy. Despite all the stories I'd heard about Barry and his coaching staff being somewhat wild and carefree, I found Barry to be a thoughtful and humorous person. He was easygoing and fun-loving.

During this period of their success, very few coaches enjoyed the same level of popularity as Barry Switzer did with OU football and Bob Knight did with IU basketball. However different their methods were, they were similar in their brilliance. Coach Knight could be every bit as personable as Barry was, and Barry could be every bit as serious and motivational with his team as Coach got the credit for being.

I remembered back at IU when Coach Knight and I would be driving somewhere, and he would always say that a good football program could be especially valuable to the basketball program. He was right. Oklahoma was bringing in millions of dollars of revenue each Saturday throughout the fall, and I had the privilege of tapping into that for my basketball program. The Sooner athletic brain trust had entrusted me with the basketball program, gave me an unlimited budget, and wanted a basketball team just like the one from Bloomington.

So did I.

Barry Switzer's post-game parties were the swell soirées of Norman, especially around 1974 and 1975 when Oklahoma won back-to-back national championships and from 1976 to 1979 when they had Heisman Trophy winner Billy Sims. If you weren't at Cross Timbers after a game, it might mean that you had been invited to Barry Switzer's house.

Oklahomans played football better than anyone else during this period—and they could celebrate pretty well, too. His parties, without a doubt, were the place to be. Attending them allowed you to meet many people you weren't going to run into any other way. The governor of Oklahoma might be there or a U.S. senator or a movie actor like James Garner. But no matter who you were, Barry made you feel welcome. I think that's why he was such a talented recruiter—he was such a good people person.

One of the first times I was at one of Barry's parties, I remember walking in and seeing author James Michener sitting on the couch. I had read many of his books, including *Centennial* and *Chesapeake*, and at the time, he was working on *Sports in America*. As I surveyed him sitting there, I think he was just as overwhelmed by the party as I was.

Things were going great in Norman. Everything was exciting, both in my professional life and my personal life.

After finishing 9-17 our first year, we had one of the biggest turnarounds in NCAA basketball our second year and finished with an 18-10 record. Our third year we finished 14-13, but it was an exciting year for me personally as Claudia and I got married. My proposal wasn't very dramatic; I just had no idea how to communicate how I felt about her after being a bachelor for so long. But she did say yes, and I was thrilled.

We got married on July 12, 1978, at Applewood Baptist Church in Wheat Ridge, Colorado. Bob Weltlich, my fellow assistant at Indiana several years before, was my best man. It was the best day of my life. Claudia and I were young and in love.

Right when it felt like life couldn't get more exciting, it did. In Claudia's first year as a coach's wife, we finished 21-10, made it to the NCAA tournament for the first time since 1947, won the Big Eight championship for the first time in the school's history, and advanced to the Sweet Sixteen only to lose to Larry Bird's Indiana State team.

That season, I would frequently look behind me during pressure-filled games and see Claudia sitting behind the bench. Seeing her there, smiling and having fun with the people around her, helped bring me back to reality. Life had more meaning because I was going through it with someone. Through the coaching highs, I could share the joy with someone who understood me better than anyone. Through the lows, I had someone who made me feel better and who I could express my frustrations to. Coaching is a fickle profession, filled with winning and losing, but Claudia would always be there. She never got too high and never got too low. She was a constant reminder to me that—no matter how the team was doing—I was, indeed, very fortunate. We were building something together. We were partners on a journey together.

The best news of the spring came two months after we advanced to the Sweet Sixteen, when Claudia and I were on one of our routine evening walks around the neighborhood.

She grabbed my hand and stopped me on the sidewalk. I remember looking at her quizzically, and noticing that she was bubbling with excitement.

"I'm pregnant," she smiled.

I was stunned at first and then absolutely thrilled, but all I could say was, "Wow, is that right?"

Remember the great scene from the *Dick Van Dyke Show* with Mary Tyler Moore, where she wakes Dick up in the middle of the night with the news that she is ready to have their baby? He immediately peels off the covers, jumps to his feet completely clothed, puts a hat on his head, and is ready to go in an instant. Claudia only wishes I would have been that prepared.

The night she went into labor, we had just lost a heartbreaker at Nebraska, where the officials had waved off a last-second shot by Bo Overton that would have won us the game (I still believe they got the call wrong). It had been a frustrating season in my fifth year at Oklahoma, and I was distraught during my flight all the way home.

She could tell when I walked into our house late that evening that I was bummed about the game. Everything that broke right for us the year before was working against us this season.

I tried to sleep it off.

Next thing I knew, it was 2 a.m., and Claudia was shaking me.

"It's time," she told me.

As I groggily sat up in bed, I mumbled, "Time for what?"

She gave me that look all wives give their husbands at some time or another.

"Oh my gosh," I finally realized, and I did my best imitation of Dick Van Dyke. "Let's go."

We drove at breakneck speed to Norman Municipal Hospital, three miles away, and four hours later, we had a seven-pound, thirteen-ounce baby boy in our arms.

I was overwhelmed by the experience. Even now, I'm not sure how to explain a moment as amazing as a child's birth. I'm lucky to have been present for all three of our kids' births, as many coaches aren't that fortunate. Each was more amazing than the one before. I couldn't stop talking about how brave my wife had been during the process. We named him Robert Brandon Bliss.

As I look back, I realize all the great things God was doing during this time of my life: first, getting the job at such a young age, then meeting Claudia, then attaining our success in basketball, and finally having a son. I was not mature enough, however, to see them as blessings, to see them as a display of God's love. I was too busy to slow down and give God His rightful credit.

Even that Friday night, as amazing as it was to witness the birth of our first child, my mind was already onto Saturday's game—a big-time afternoon television game against Kansas State for first place in our conference.

The television people had gone to the hospital before the game to do a segment on our child's birth, and poor Claudia had to try her best to look presentable when all she wanted to do, I'm sure, was sleep and recover.

Before the game, in a neat gesture, our Oklahoma cheerleaders had passed out cigars to the sellout crowd in honor of our son's arrival. Needless to say, it makes you feel appreciated when the entire arena—10,000 strong—is celebrating the birth of your son. Things had certainly changed since our first season when less than a thousand people showed up at our games. This was the excitement and energy we wanted Oklahoma basketball to have. We had done the unimaginable: We filled the LNC without wrestling.

With forty seconds left, Kansas State was ahead by three and had its eighty-percent free throw shooter, Rolando Blackman, on the line with a chance to secure the victory for them. He missed the front end of the one-and-one attempt, however, and our star forward Terry Stotts—from Bloomington, Indiana, of all places—got the rebound, ran the ball down the floor, and nailed a seventeen-footer to get us within a point (we didn't have a three-point shot in college hoops at this time). We called a timeout immediately with about twenty seconds remaining.

Upon inbounding the ball, one of their guards inadvertently stepped out of bounds, and we got the ball back under our basket. Stotts inbounded the ball to our point guard Raymond Whitley, who barely missed a ten-footer, but Aaron Curry grabbed the weak-side offensive rebound and scored to give us a one-point lead. Four timeouts ensued, and they missed a game-winning shot at the buzzer. We ran up the ramp to the locker room, high-fiving and embracing our fans the entire way. It was a special moment. We were back in first place and I was a father—could it get any better?

In the locker room, I remember Terry Stotts saying the post-game prayer and then speaking to the players and coaches as he held the game ball, "This is a birthday present for Robert Brandon Bliss."

I gave him a big kiss on the cheek.

07

MUSTANG

During the fall of 1978, I was in Dallas, Texas, recruiting for our OU team, and I had a couple of hours free. I decided to drop by Southern Methodist University (SMU) to meet Russ Potts, who was one of the new breed of athletic directors on the cutting edge of marketing and promotion in college athletics. I had been thinking that we needed to take advantage of our great success the year before with some type of marketing campaign, but since Russ Potts was already implementing this strategy in a big fashion in Dallas, for his home-standing SMU Mustangs, I decided it would be wise to talk with him.

Whether it was a slogan, a billboard, or a game promotion, SMU's "Mustang Mania" was seen all over the Metroplex. At the same time, Potts hired an outgoing young man, Ron Meyer, as his football coach. Meyer, in turn, recruited some of the best football talent in the country, and Mustang Mania was off and running. I was duly impressed.

On the visit to SMU, I wanted to gain some ideas that I could take back to Norman and implement with our Sooner basketball team. In a nutshell, we eventually used a lot of the Mustang-bred ideas during the 1980 season, but I also became very good friends with Russ Potts.

Our 1979 Sooner season had started out with a lot of promise, but after the great win against Kansas State (the day after Rob was born) put us in first place, we fizzled down the stretch. This made me start to think about my future at Oklahoma. We had been there five years—were we getting better or had we peaked?

Fast forward to late that same season and word came through the *Dallas Morning News* that Sonny Allen, the personable basketball coach at SMU, would not be returning to the Hilltop. I didn't think much about it until Russ Potts called me at home just a few days later and asked if I would be interested in talking to him regarding the Mustang position.

Over that next weekend I discussed the offer with my two confidants, Claudia and Doug Ash. Claudia was so busy with Robert that she was leaving it in my hands, but Doug was equally intrigued. He reminded me how much we had liked playing in Moody Coliseum in the NCAA tournament the year before. And Doug also made a good case for developing a quality basketball program in Dallas because of the level of basketball players that seemed to be now available in Texas. And, of course, we had witnessed the recruiting success Barry Switzer's football team was having south of the Red River.

Looking back, I remember Coach Knight telling me that he would help me obtain my first head coaching job, but my performance in that first job would determine my next opportunity. So, although Bob Knight taught me how to coach, Oklahoma had thrown me into the fire and we had survived. This newfound confidence was strange, but when SMU offered to double my Oklahoma salary, I took it as a sign that I should move on to Dallas and coach the Ponies. Money isn't always a good reason to change jobs, but that was a nice raise for newlyweds with a three-month old son. Plus, I thought that if we had been able to build a good program at OU, we could certainly do it at SMU. It was a great school, and we were located in Dallas—a recruiting hotbed.

We accepted the job on a Thursday, and they wanted to have a press conference on Friday afternoon, so we quickly packed our bags for the three-hour drive down to Dallas.

I couldn't help but think how different my life was five years earlier when I accepted the OU job. Now, I had my beautiful wife in the passenger seat and my three-month old son in his car seat in the back.

At one point in the drive, we pulled over to get a soda. While we were stopped, Claudia decided to change Rob's diaper. She put him on the center console of the car and removed his diaper. At that moment, for some reason, Rob decided to relieve himself and a little fountain of urine rose and fell right in my drink.

Claudia and I looked at each other, shocked, but then burst into laughter. Rob kicked his little legs. Part of me thinks he knew exactly what he did. Maybe he didn't want to leave Oklahoma.

Claudia and I loved being in Dallas from the very start, but the first couple of basketball seasons at SMU were worse than our start at Oklahoma. We finished 7-20 the first year and the second year was even worse at 6-21. There was no Coach of the Year award to help boost our morale or the Mustang fans' confidence in their young hire. We had pretty much cleaned house and recruited brand-new players, but they weren't quite ready to play in the competitive Southwest Conference. If I would have had back-to-back years like that in this day of coaching, I might have been fired. SMU had been struggling before I got there, but not that badly. And so, for the first time as a coach, I considered the possibility that my job might be in jeopardy.

My response to losing games was always to work harder. So that's what we did. We stayed in the office later. We ordered more carryout. We watched more film. We had more player conferences. We slept less.

Working harder isn't necessarily a bad thing, but it can become a snare if it warps your priorities. And, though my priorities might have been slowly getting out of whack, it didn't keep us from excelling professionally. I think this is a subtle danger of any striving—in the short run it can result in success. What happens in the long run, many times, depends on the character of the person involved.

Thankfully, we won nineteen games our third year—one of the biggest turnarounds in college basketball. All our young guys were playing well. Jon Koncak, Butch Moore, Larry Davis, and Carl Wright were all "coming of age." And by the fourth year, we had really started to mesh, as we finished 25-8 and made the NCAA tournament, SMU's first appearance since 1967. We defeated Miami (Ohio) in the first round, but then lost in the next round to Patrick Ewing and the Georgetown Hoyas. Our young team played a fantastic game, even leading the Hoyas at intermission, 24-16, but Georgetown came back in the second half to defeat us 37-36. Georgetown then went on to win the national title, ours the only really close game John Thompson's talented team had in the tournament.

Just like Oklahoma, it took us four years to restore the program and get back to the NCAA tournament. And just like Oklahoma, the basketball program was often overshadowed by other sports. In Oklahoma, it was football. At SMU, our football was pretty good, too, but it was the city's newly acquired Dallas Mavericks that provided the most competition. But, nevertheless, there was excitement in Dallas for college basketball again.

The following season (1985) was another great year, and during this two-year period the Mustangs had beaten such recognized national programs—Duke, North Carolina, Louisville, Kentucky, Houston, Oklahoma, and Arkansas. At one point during the season, in the middle of February, we were ranked No. 2 in the country with Georgetown No. 1. If I remember correctly, we had a chance to capture the top spot after Georgetown lost in the afternoon, but we got beat at the buzzer by Texas Tech that evening. As a head coach, it was the closest I ever came to having the top-ranked team in the country.

Although the Ponies were ranked in the Top Ten for most of the year, the conclusion of our season was a real disappointment. With another made-for-television appearance vs. Georgetown looming ahead in the second round of the NCAA tournament, we dropped a tough first-round game to a hustling Loyola outfit, and our season ended with a 23-10 record.

We struggled the next two years and didn't make the NCAA tournament with an 18-11 record in Year 6 and a 16-13 record in Year 7. During those two years, however, Doug and the coaches put together one of my favorite teams in my three decades of coaching—the 1988 SMU team—a team that, I believe, had some of the most talented guards in the country.

All summer of the 1988 offseason, I traveled the basketball clinic circuit listening to Rick Pitino talk about his "Black-White, Box-Diamond Press." I had watched how he utilized the press and the three-point shot with his Providence team, driving them all the way to the Final Four in 1987. Providence not only was successful, but they were fun to watch. I felt like we had a similar team when it came to our guards and athleticism.

I would attend a clinic, listen to Coach Pitino lecture, find him afterward, and pick his brain about the specifics of the press. At the next clinic, he would look up into the stands and see me again. After he was done teaching, I would do the exact same thing. Find him. Bombard him with questions.

We implemented what I learned from Rick Pitino, and the result was a 28-5 record, the most wins in SMU's basketball history. We won both the Southwest Conference regular season title and the postseason conference tournament (SMU's first Southwest Conference tournament title), and we defeated Notre Dame on St. Patrick's Day in the first round of the NCAA tournament. We faced Duke, the No. 1 seed in the second round, and, again, lost to a team that would end up playing in the Final Four.

Our days in Dallas were golden.

There may have been some doubts from the Mustang faithful our first two seasons, but the following years were some of the most exciting in the program's history.

During those eight years, Claudia and I also had two more children: a daughter, Berkeley, and another son, Jeff. Claudia was great at taking care of our three children. I loved being a father and spending the offseason with our family.

Whatever the American dream was, it felt like we were living it.

STRIVING

Something else happened to me in Dallas—something that could have been a pivotal moment in my life but wasn't; something that could have changed my thinking, but didn't.

Upon taking the Southern Methodist University job in early 1980, Claudia and I moved to a beautiful area in north Dallas. Not long after getting settled, we were looking for a church home, and, since she was Baptist, we settled on an amazing church called Park Cities Baptist Church.

This was good for me, and it was good for us. On November 1, 1980, I sat in Pastor James Pleitz's office as he led me through the Sinner's Prayer and I accepted Jesus Christ as my Savior. I had only been a Baptist for a few years, but I knew this was an important step.

But, as I look back, although I had accepted Jesus Christ as my Savior, I hadn't accepted Him as Lord. I had accepted "salvation," but I had no idea about a thing called "surrender."

One writer's analogy of a "Christian streaker" fit me perfectly. I was aimlessly running around with my "helmet of salvation"—but nothing else. I was the lord of my own life. I was taught about eternity, but I didn't know how to live on earth.

Although I would sometimes thank God for the good things that were happening around me, I didn't alter my lifestyle to reflect any form of surrender. In fact, probably quite the opposite was occurring. I was experiencing some successes and was willing to take all the credit. This all fed into my thinking that I was doing pretty well for myself. As the early success at Oklahoma paved the way for a good run in Dallas at SMU, my life philosophy was developing . . . and not all of it was good.

Although I professed to be a believer of Jesus Christ, I wasn't a follower, and my actions certainly showed it. After all, didn't even the demons believe in Jesus? But they didn't follow Him. True believers follow Jesus because they are awakened to the deep and sincere love He has for them. This concept of following Christ escaped me because I was unaware of the extent of His love, a love that has the ability to shape, mold, and convict.

In looking back, the reason I think I claimed Christianity at all throughout my life was because it made me feel good and seemed to be the right thing to do. As a man, I always wanted to be thought of as a good person, but what did all of that entail? To me, it probably meant you were a good father, and you were faithful to your wife.

I wanted to be thought of as a good Christian man, so I guess that I played the part. Over the years—through West Point, Indiana, Oklahoma, and SMU—I believe I became an "a la carte christian," and yes, I use a lowercase "c" purposely because I was a poor excuse for a capital "C" Christian. Instead of establishing a relationship with Jesus, it was like I was completing a religious inventory checklist:

Church attendance: check.

Bible study: check again.

FCA camp: check.

Power lunch: check.

Youth rally: check.

I am definitely not saying that it wasn't good to be involved in these pursuits, but not with the self-serving intentions I apparently had. It is said that some people base their conduct on their theology, and that probably means they honor Christ through the actions of their lives. I am afraid that I was the opposite. It seems that I had slowly developed my theology around my conduct, similar to what the last sentence in Judges says: "Everyone did what was right in their own eyes."

I would use my Christianity and wear it like a new suit—it made me look good and feel good. Like a hypocritical politician, my version of religion wasn't much more than a marketing approach. I had failed to understand what "God's love" was all about, and what "Jesus" was all about.

The reality is that God gave me my capabilities and gifts at birth, but most of my career had been spent simply "striving after the wind." I never gave God enough credit for supplying my "gifts," nor did I realize that Jesus' death on the cross had more meaning than just salvation.

My spiritual insecurity, because of my ignorance of God's love, combined with my performance-driven personality, were deadly inoculants that were evident in my appearance and conduct.

Simply put, I was a typical male, meaning I was performance-driven and overly conscious of people's opinions of me.

And even scarier, I was a typical Christian—unconscious of God's love.

09
LOBO

Our historic 1988 season at SMU had just ended, and we had just returned from the NCAA tournament games in Chapel Hill, North Carolina. I was in Dallas straightening things up around the office before we set out for spring recruiting.

My phone rang. It was Claudia.

Initially, I was concerned because it was nine o'clock in the morning, and she was always too busy with our three children to call that early. As I answered the phone, however, I could tell she was excited.

She went on to tell me that her mother, Jay Fosnes, had just called from Albuquerque to tell her that the head coaching position at the University of New Mexico had opened up and that I should take it because she (Jay) could see her grandchildren more often. She said it just that way, as if all you have to do is call and the job would be ours. Snap your fingers. Pick a job. As easy as that.

I certainly wasn't looking for another job because we were returning almost the entire roster from a team that had won twenty-eight games. And yet, I was intrigued. Claudia's parents had retired to the Albuquerque area, home of UNM, several years before. Claudia's sister, her husband, and their four children also lived there. And I had always been impressed with the home court of the Lobos, University Arena, better known as The Pit. For several years, The Pit had been ranked in the Top Ten in college basketball attendance, seating an average just under 18,000. And when the fans got "wired" cheering for the hometown Lobos, it featured a decibel level just under that of a jet airplane. Doug and I had never coached in a setting like that.

The more I thought about it, the more it appealed to me.

I mentioned it later that morning to Doug Ash. Doug always looked at schools very objectively. At the end of the day, every coach looks at a program with a couple of thoughts in mind: Can we get players to go there, and can we win the conference and get to the NCAA tournament? Doug believed, as I did, that it would be a great place to coach.

The next morning, I made some initial inquiries about the job, and everything seemed extremely positive, especially coming off the season we just had at SMU. But then I heard something that made me really sit up and take notice.

Someone else was also interested in the Lobo head-coaching job—none other than my mentor, Bob Knight.

UNM Athletic Director John Koenig placed a couple of calls to Bloomington, and it soon became the talk of college basketball: Bob Knight might be leaving IU for the Southwest. In the meantime, I had also received my own call from Mr. Koenig. He was very polite and expressed interest, but I was a realist. If Coach wanted the job at New Mexico, it was his.

A couple of days later, I was giving a clinic in Memphis, Tennessee, when I received a call from Coach Knight. He asked me, "You interested in the New Mexico job?"

"I really am," I answered. I wanted to tell him that Claudia's mom would be mad at him if he took the job, but I didn't.

"How about we meet in New Orleans this Friday?" he suggested. "I am going to a clinic, and we can discuss the job."

I arrived at a hotel in downtown New Orleans and sat in the back of his clinic, as I had done so many times before. I once again marveled at his ability to make the game simple. After he finished, we went upstairs and sat in his hotel room. After a few pleasantries, he broke it all down for me. Sure, he had always thought of taking another job sometime, but he knew he had it pretty good at IU. He was having difficulties with his president, however, and was much more serious about the prospect of leaving Bloomington than I ever imagined. These were the warning signs, I believe, to the travesty that eventually unfolded at Indiana—the warning signs that Coach would eventually be terribly mistreated when he was let go in 2000.

Bob Knight loved Indiana. In my opinion, Bloomington should have been his home for his entire life, and Hoosier fans should be able to show up on his doorstep every day and pay their respects. I know, without a doubt, he would talk to each and every one of them. By this point, he had led them to three national titles, and when things were beginning to turn sour, it was only a year after his most recent title in 1987, which is kind of revealing itself.

Nevertheless, Bob confessed to me that he didn't feel comfortable leaving Indiana yet. He felt there was still work to do, so he would turn the job down and recommend that they hire me, which is what happened.

After New Mexico finally hired me, some writers asked me if I was bothered that I was UNM's second choice. I joked with them, "No, it didn't bother me because I was my wife's second choice, too." *Sports Illustrated* carried the quote in their "They Said It" column, and we had some laughs.

New Mexico was a great family move. And I felt fortunate to even be in a position where I could make a move that was good for my family and still keep doing what I loved to do: coach basketball. I had never had that luxury as a coach before, and many coaches don't. Not that I was a hot commodity, but I had developed a respectable reputation between Oklahoma and SMU, and everything seemed to align at just the right time.

Robert had just turned eight, Berkeley would soon be seven, and Jeffrey was two. We would spend the next eleven years in Albuquerque raising our children in the greatest setting a man could ever ask for. Being in the same city as the kids' grandparents, aunt, uncle, and cousins was a blessing. I loved seeing our extended family on a weekly and sometimes daily basis.

Claudia would take all the children to The Pit, and they would run around the arena playing hide-and-seek or some such chase game. They would come with me to basketball camps and would help me with the concession stand. It was a great time to be the coach in Albuquerque, and we took every advantage of it.

For the first time, I began to believe that I might end my career coaching where I was, for the Lobos in Albuquerque.

Doug Ash and I went right to work. Our first season, we finished with a 22-11 record and a tie for second place in the Western Athletic Conference (WAC). Our second year we finished 20-14. The third year we got over the hump, so to speak, and took UNM to its first NCAA tournament in thirteen years.

Again, we felt like we had accomplished what we had set out to do—restore the program, continue bringing excitement to The Pit, and get to the NCAA tournament. We felt like we were flying high, just like we had done at SMU and just like we had done at Oklahoma. To watch each school get excited about basketball again was exhilarating for us—it was a feeling that coaches craved.

We went to the NIT the following year, but we made it back to the NCAA tournament six out of our final seven years at New Mexico. Our first three times we were eliminated in the first round. Our next four times, we were eliminated in the second round. Overall, we won four NCAA tournament games. We were the WAC champions in the 1993-94 season and tournament champs in the 1992-93 and 1995-96 seasons.

In 1999, our last season at New Mexico, we finished with a 25-9 record and finished second in the WAC. We earned another trip to the NCAA tournament (our seventh in nine years), where we gave Missouri a loss in Norm Stewart's final game as a coach. The next game was against No. 1-seeded University of Connecticut. We were really looking forward to this game because it was in Denver,

Claudia's hometown, and we had a lot of friends at the game.

For some reason, however, it appeared as if our players were tight, and UConn pulled ahead early. We battled back but still lost by twenty points. UConn went on to win the national championship, similar to what Georgetown had done to us fifteen years earlier. That's the problem with having the No. 8 or No. 9 seed, which we had several times at New Mexico. We could get by the first game, but the next game was usually against a No. 1 seed, and they always seemed to get us.

My salary had once again doubled during my time at UNM. Part of this is natural, as the longer you do something, the more money you will typically make. But part of it also shows how sports-saturated and money-driven the culture of college athletics was becoming.

Also, when a six-figure salary is thrown at you, it is easy for your perspective to get warped and for you to lose focus and to feel as important as the money indicates. It doesn't happen overnight; it's gradual. It comes down to the condition of the heart.

I never planned on leaving New Mexico because it was an ideal situation for our family. I dearly loved the school. Doug and I talked a great deal about New Mexico being our last stop, but when Baylor University athletic director Tom Stanton called and offered me the head-coaching job with the Bears, I listened.

Eleven years at one place is a long time. Maybe it was time to look at something else? The more I thought about it, the more appealing the Baylor opportunity sounded. After talking it over with Claudia and getting Doug's feedback, it was decided. Our next stop would be Baylor University in Waco, Texas.

Actually, this would turn out to be our final stop—but for reasons I never expected.

PART 2

ASHES

10

IMPERFECT STORM

In the spring, at the time when kings go off to war, David sent Joab out with the king's men and the whole Israelite army. They destroyed the Ammonites and besieged Rabbah. But David remained in Jerusalem.

2 Samuel 11:1 (NIV)

One of the very best biographies on King David is Chuck Swindoll's *David: A Man of Passion and Destiny*. In setting the stage for David's adultery with Bathsheba, Swindoll says:

Look at his (David's) track record. A humble beginning. A giant killer. Two decades of sterling leadership. Choice men in the right places. A military force every foe respected. Enlarged boundaries that now reached 60,000 square miles. No defeats on the battlefield. Exports, imports, strong national defense, financial health, a beautiful new home, plans for the temple of the Lord.

Things were definitely going well for King David. Perhaps he had earned the right to relax at home while all of his Israelite army "destroyed the Ammonites and besieged Rabbah," as 2 Samuel 11:1 says above.

The text implies David was so secure on his throne that he no longer felt he had to prove his military prowess. Instead, he could place the responsibility on his generals. This demonstrated his extreme confidence and security. And although David had not technically done anything "wrong," the state of his heart would soon be revealed. There is an overarching sense to the reader that David is doomed—that his internal spiritual temperature (his ignorance or forgetfulness of God's love and perhaps his lofty opinion of himself) will set him up for a monstrous fall.

When an ignorant man wanders through an imperfect world, calamity is always on the horizon.

Although we were leaving the safe haven of Albuquerque, our extended family, and New Mexico Lobo Basketball—with its loyal fans and twenty-win seasons—I was excited to return to Texas. There were three factors that played into my excitement about going to Baylor University.

First, I loved Texas. As the expression goes, "I wasn't born in Texas, but I got there as fast as I could." "Fast" turned out to be 1980 when I took the Southern Methodist University job in Dallas. After eight good years in Dallas, we went to the University of New Mexico for the next eleven years. But I always loved Texas. Despite its scalding summers (I never enjoyed a cold climate), I loved the weather and loved the people with their never-say-die spirit.

Second, I also was looking forward to competing in the Big 12, a great basketball league. The Western Athletic Conference (WAC) was a great league, too, but competitive people always enjoy competing against the best, and during the late 1990s, the Big 12 was one of the best.

The third reason was that I had always thought that I might end my coaching career at a small Christian school, but now I had the opportunity of coaching at the largest Baptist school in the world. I felt that perhaps God had created this "opportunity" for me—or was I trying to add it to my checklist? And the fact that they were going to pay me more than twice what I was making in Albuquerque sweetened the deal. All that said, I imagine that a lot of people thought that leaving Albuquerque was a questionable move, but I was excited to get started.

Our first year at Baylor, however, was all about survival, both with my family and with our team. My family was excited about coming to Waco, but I knew there were times that they were wondering what we had done. We had left a tremendous support base in Albuquerque.

Our Baylor Bears tried hard in Year 1, and, although they had lost sixteen straight conference games the previous season, they were giving us a great effort. We started with a 9-2 record during non-conference play, including a nice win against Marquette. The first three conference games, however, all resulted in losses by an average of twenty-five points. Welcome to the Big 12.

We bounced back to defeat Texas Tech in Waco, the team's first conference victory in over a year, and unceremoniously finished the season with a 14-15 record. A win in the Big 12 tournament against Nebraska served to create a little excitement leading into our second campaign in 2000.

More important, we showed signs of what we could be.

Year 2 at Baylor displayed many of the same positive signs we had experienced at our other stops, hints that success was on the horizon. As a coach, I derived a great deal of pleasure out of "untangling the knot."

We started the season with a perfect 11-0 record and could see energy slowly returning to Baylor basketball. Then, on a "Fill the Ferrell Center" promotion, we defeated Colorado in front of a sellout crowd, 61-56, for our twelfth win of the year.

Several weeks later, in early February, we had another crucial contest: an ESPN "Big Monday" showdown with No. 5 Kansas at home. It was Baylor's first appearance on ESPN's "Big Monday" game, and it was against a Kansas team many believed could win the national championship.

Most people didn't believe we stood a chance against Kansas. After all, Baylor hadn't defeated a Top Ten team in eleven years. Kansas was more talented, more experienced, more confident, and coached by one of the very best coaches in college basketball: Roy Williams. Apparently, some of the Jayhawk players didn't think we stood a chance, either; after Kansas's previous loss to Iowa State earlier that week, Jayhawk guard Kenny Gregory was quoted as saying, "It's not like we lost to Baylor." I have to admit that the comment did make it up on our bulletin board.

I remember talking to our coaches as we were preparing our game plan and telling them I thought our only advantage might be our athletic ability. Kansas was athletic and played quickly, too, but I felt we might be a little quicker overall. I knew we didn't want to let them control the tempo of the game, so we told our point guard, DeMarcus Minor, to "push" the ball at every opportunity. I didn't want us to play like wimps in our first appearance on Big Monday.

At halftime, we led No. 5 Kansas by twenty-five points.

Our forward Terry Black had a number of ferocious dunks in the first half and was quickly establishing himself as one of the most exciting players in the country. The Ferrell Center was absolutely electric, but as we walked into the locker room at half time, I remember telling Doug Ash, "We might not be far enough ahead."

Kansas was *that* good.

We faltered a bit in the second half, but hung on for an encouraging 85-77 win against a Kansas team that included five future NBA players. Coach Williams, always a classy coach, told me after the game at the handshake that he was disappointed they lost, but happy that our players played well for us.

Kansas was the highest-ranked opponent the Bears had defeated since 1990 when they upset No. 3-ranked Arkansas. Our victory seemed to be a declaration that, although Baylor basketball had a ways to go, we were at least headed in the right direction. We had accomplished something significant, and the locals were excited.

When I walked into my office on Tuesday morning, I saw a small note card on my desk. I picked it up. It was a hand-written note from Baylor's president, Robert Sloan. He complimented us on the win and said he admired my ability to work with young people.

Earlier that same morning I had also been invited to be on the morning national talk show, *Mike & Mike,* a show that was in its infancy. Numerous articles were published in newspapers across the country about our victory, but it was President Sloan's note that meant the most to me. It reaffirmed everything I was trying to do at Baylor. I enjoyed being thought of as someone who could get a team together and teach them to accomplish great things. His note let me know that he was pleased that he hired us.

I put the note on my shelf and had a special moment there alone in my office. The victory over Kansas was a confirmation that we were right where we were supposed to be, and I was very proud of what our program was becoming.

We finished the regular season schedule with a 6-10 record, but we were playing pretty well—just in the wrong conference. The Big 12 tournament in Kansas City was next, and we beat Colorado again in overtime in the opening round, setting up a rematch against league champion Iowa State. This was a team that had its way with us earlier in the season, defeating us 72-51 in Ames, Iowa.

We knew the rematch would be a challenge, but we were excited about having another shot at them. The two-time defending Big 12 regular season champions were ranked No. 7 in the country, and many prognosticators were now picking them as a possible Final Four team. Doug and I always prided ourselves, however, on our ability to make adjustments, one game to the next. The problem was that we only had a few hours to prepare after our Colorado win for Iowa State's "penetrate and kick" offense led by

All-American Jamaal Tinsley.

We told our players to focus on our gapping defense, specifically on drawing charges, and by halftime, we had held Iowa State to nineteen points and had taken five charges that got some of their best players in foul trouble. Our defense had completely disrupted their entire game plan. We never allowed the game to get close and won 62-49—another victory against a Top Ten team in the country. As the eighth seed, it was the biggest upset in Big 12 tournament history, sending 12,000 Iowa State fans back home. Plus, it was a thirty-four-point turnaround against a Top Ten team, no small feat.

Unfortunately, we lost to Texas in the Big 12 semifinals, thus ending our hopes of making a miracle NCAA tournament run. But we did earn a bid to the NIT, which was a step in the right direction for the Baylor program. When it became apparent that we were NIT-bound, I had a hunch who our first-round opponent would be—and I was right. We were told that we would be playing the New Mexico Lobos . . . in Albuquerque . . . at The Pit.

The media seemed to latch onto the obvious storyline: "Bliss Back in The Pit." It was much more than a basketball game to me, and I was excited to return to The Pit simply because it's The Pit. After all, we had a lot of great memories in Albuquerque. And I confess: It was weird walking down the ramp and taking a seat on the visitor bench after all those years on the home bench. Some of my old friends really let me have it as I walked onto the court with my team.

The game came down to the wire, but New Mexico pulled off an 83-73 victory. Our players really played hard and wanted to win the game for Doug and me, but I left the floor grateful for the season we had. We were excited about our future.

After the game, as I shook hands with all the New Mexico players, I made it a point to compliment one player for his spirited game against us.

His name was Patrick Dennehy.

During the offseason of 2001, the NCAA implemented something called the "5/8 Rule," which restricted programs to eight scholarships over a two-year period but only five scholarships in one year. The rule was instituted to help graduation rates and encourage coaches to recruit players who wanted to stay in school for the duration and earn their degree with their respective school. If you want to read between the lines, however, it was really instituted because coaches were running players out of their programs to make room for other better players.

I remember the previous year when I was at the National Association of Basketball Coaches summer meeting as the rule was being discussed. Most coaches disliked it because it handcuffed them. Both Roy Williams and Bob Knight, two of the best coaches in the country, publicly expressed their disdain for the rule. And apparently they were right, because in April 2004, the rule was discontinued.

At the time, the rule had no effect on Baylor.

But it would.

Year 3 didn't go as well as Year 2.

We had another great win in an ESPN Big Monday game against Missouri, but the season never matched the intensity of the previous year. We graduated both Terry Black and DeMarcus Minor, and I hoped our three transfers would help us pick up right where we left off. That wasn't the case. We finished with a 14-15 overall regular season record and a 4-12 conference record. The regular season ended in heartbreaking fashion: a 91-89 loss to Texas Tech coached by none other than Bob Knight, who had taken over the Red Raiders head coaching reins that year. We followed that with a first-round loss in the Big 12 tournament. Unlike the previous year, we didn't even make the NIT.

The only highlight of the year was a personal one. Doug and I achieved our 500th career victory in a late-November game against Texas-Arlington. I was the thirty-first Division I head coach to reach the milestone. Not bad for someone who thirty-five years prior thought he was going to be a P&G salesman.

But the accomplishment didn't last long in my mind. I hardly enjoyed the moment. I was consumed in the ups and downs of our season. After all the success we had the previous season, it felt like we had taken several steps backward.

As the season progressed, I was starting to feel more and more uncomfortable with our inability to get better. Our third year, typically, was our turning point in building a program; at Oklahoma, we had gone 18-10, after a 9-17 first year; at SMU, we finished 19-11 in the third year after going 7-20 and 6-21 the first two seasons; and at New Mexico, we made the NCAA tournament after making the NIT the first two seasons. Lack of improvement was not something I was accustomed to.

I felt we had good players, but I was frustrated that I couldn't get them to play better. I didn't know what else to do but to work harder. Twenty-seven years into my head coaching career, I was working harder than I ever had before, and I was hungrier for success than ever before.

The only way a performance-driven person can react is to work harder. Nobody in the Baylor administration indicated any displeasure with the program. But as crazy as it sounds, I really think I had become captive of our own success. I was convinced that the only thing that could free me from this frustration was winning more—improving my performance. In looking back, it became obvious that my performance was how I determined my worth.

At the end of Year 3, we made a few moves that we felt were necessary in order to upgrade our program.

First, we hired a young assistant named Rodney Belcher, who had been a successful high school coach in Dallas and was active in the summer basketball circles. I had been impressed with Rodney when I had seen him on the recruiting trail, and since we recruited the Metroplex thoroughly, we felt he would be a good addition to our program.

Secondly, I approached the administration to see if we could get some relief from Baylor's high academic standards. I didn't want to bring in bad students; I just wanted to get some consideration on borderline cases. I could justify it in my mind because the other head coaches in our conference were recruiting these same players. After all, we were the only private school in a league full of state schools. I felt we were already at a disadvantage, and I just wanted to try to level the playing field. Baylor trusted me and gave me some leeway.

I sincerely appreciated that Baylor was willing to trust me in bringing in quality recruits, even though they weren't great students. So we recruited a couple of junior college players, who weren't bad students, but would enter Baylor under a watchful eye. These junior college players would help us maintain our quickness since we had lost a bit of our athleticism. However, as the year progressed, it became apparent that they would need summer school in 2003 to become eligible.

Thirdly, in late spring, we lost sophomore Logan Kosmalski, a steady power forward who helped our team overachieve in Year 2. Kosmalski, disappointed that he had to share time in Year 3 with Lawrence Roberts, a talented freshman, left the program. Hastily, we went after and signed Carlton Dotson from Paris Junior College as a backup for Lawrence.

Carlton Dotson was now a Baylor Bear.

Earlier that year, I had been selected as the coach of the Big 12 All-Star team that was invited that summer to play basketball in Sweden, Norway, and Denmark. Since Claudia was of Scandinavian descent, it seemed like a great opportunity to go on a family trip. Before we left, however, I was informed that three of our junior college players were in jeopardy of failing to complete their summer school requirements.

It was about this time that a fourth occurrence presented itself: We heard that Patrick Dennehy might not be returning to the University of New Mexico. Because we were concerned about our numbers and athletic ability, Rodney suggested we look at Patrick.

Patrick was an impressive young man, and although we knew he wouldn't be eligible for a year, he was too good a prospect to turn down. Doug, Rodney, and I also felt that a change of scenery might be good for him. We knew that he had some disciplinary issues at UNM, but we still recruited him. And we were successful.

Patrick Dennehy was now a Baylor Bear.

Then, in late August, a fifth situation occurred. We made the difficult decision to cut guard Wendell Greenleaf because of some poor choices on social issues. The combination of losing Wendell and the uncertainty of our three junior college players in summer school made me panic. When I looked at our once-promising roster, I realized that if we lost all three of our summer school players, not only would we not have enough players but we wouldn't be very athletic, either. We needed more players, and we needed them quickly.

With this in mind, we recruited a player named Corey Herring. He was a good student from prep school and, although not a great offensive player, we felt like he would help add some athleticism.

Corey Herring was now a Baylor Bear.

The first day of school came, and all of a sudden, things began to happen very fast. Much too fast.

First, we learned that all three of our junior college players in summer school had miraculously passed, making them eligible for the season. On one hand, this was good; we wanted them to pass, obviously, but we had heard there wasn't much chance. Now we had a problem.

Remember the "5/8 Rule" that was implemented the previous offseason by the NCAA? The rule limited us to five scholarship players in one year. We had calculated for this before—we had our three junior college players in summer school and two incoming freshmen filling these five slots. But when we heard all three of our junior college players were struggling in summer school, we added both Dennehy and Herring as backups. When all three of our junior college players passed, this put us at seven scholarships in one year. Now, our roster looked like this (the asterisks indicate our seven newcomers):

1. Lawrence Roberts
2. John Lucas
3. Kenny Taylor
4. R.T. Guinn
5. Matt Sayman
6. Steven Othoro
7. Carlton Dotson *
8. Terrance Thomas *
9. Ellis Kidd *
10. Tommy Swanson *
11. Robert Hart *
12. Patrick Dennehy *
13. Cory Herring *

This was precisely what the coaches were protesting about the previous summer. Although we were completely in line with the thirteen-scholarship limit, the additions of Dennehy and Herring put us at seven "new" players in one year. Since the rule only allowed us to have five new scholarship players in one year, it put me in a quandary. What would we do with Dennehy and Herring? We had welcomed them to Baylor with open arms and promised their parents we would look after them, so I felt guilty reneging on my word—especially with the school year just beginning.

I was reminded by the coaches on my staff, however, that both of the players might be able to qualify for the different financial aid packages available at most schools. Programs like Pell Grant, Stafford Loans, etc., might help them pay their own way at Baylor.

This happens at programs all around the country, and the players become known as "walk-ons." They are not technically on scholarship, but by paying their own way, they can be part of the team.

I had to make some hard decisions and I had to make them quickly because school had started. Do I cut the two recruits loose or try to find financial aid for them?

I decided to keep them.

The coaching pride in me knew that I needed them, too. As competitive as I was, I couldn't bear to continue losing talent. Once Dennehy's redshirt transfer year was over, I knew he could probably start for Baylor. There was no way I could cut someone with that much talent. I would figure out a way to keep them. Coaches make split-second decisions every day based on what they feel is best for their program. Then they attempt to make the decision fit into reality. Our program needed to improve.

I immediately set out to try to find financial aid for them. It soon was obvious that the families were not going to be able to help, so I inquired about the different loans and scholarships at the school's financial aid office. I even went to a local bank, The First National Bank of Central Texas, and talked to a young lady in the loan department. I did not have any success.

And, though I had not yet done anything wrong, I knew that once I made the decision to keep them, the die had been cast.

This is the coach's way. Make a quick decision; then try to make it work.

There was no turning back.

Pastor and author Charles Stanley cautions never to make important decisions when you are in a HALT (hungry, angry, lonely, or tired) mentality. I wasn't hungry or angry or lonely, but I was tired because I was working harder than ever before. This emotional state had allowed me to become desensitized. Much like King David, this desensitization occurred because of my past success, which earned me trust without accountability.

When I saw the amount that needed to be paid for Dennehy and Herring, I could tell immediately that it was going to be difficult for them to find enough money to pay it. Even with financial aid. Even with a loan. Baylor, being a private school, was appreciably more expensive than the state schools I had been at previously (Oklahoma and New Mexico).

But I made the decision in such haste and in a fatigued state that I approached it with a "We'll figure it out later" mentality, when, in reality, there was no realistic, legal way to come up with the money. Almost immediately, I questioned what I had done.

The 2003 season was an absolute blur. I had not technically done anything wrong—yet—though I knew deep down that the decision to keep Dennehy and Herring was a foolish one. If I had thought about the decision for even one day longer, I wonder if I would have kept them?

Now I was trapped and I knew it.

During the fall, the Financial Aid office called me two or three times, requesting that they make their tuition payments, but I kept putting them off, saying the players' families were working on it. I continued to try to figure some legitimate way for them to pay their tuition.

The calls continued throughout the winter and with each call, I began to feel worse and worse. The hope of finding a legitimate financial source for Dennehy and Herring was looking increasingly unrealistic.

And I knew where it was possibly heading.

11
BATHSHEBA

One evening David got up from his bed and walked around on the roof of the palace. From the roof he saw a woman bathing. The woman was very beautiful and David sent someone to find out about her. The man said, "She is Bathsheba, the daughter of Eliam and the wife of Uriah the Hittite." Then David sent messengers to get her. She came to him, and he slept with her.

2 Samuel 11:2-4a (NIV)

When Texas Tech hired Bob Knight the previous March, I knew one thing was certain: Baylor would have at least two games a year against my mentor, and after going twenty-seven years without ever playing him, I didn't look forward to it at all. There were a few people I just didn't like to play against because they were my friends, and I knew how important it was for each of us to win the game. Bob Knight was at the top of my list.

After losing to Coach and his Red Raiders, 70-64, earlier that year, we ended the regular season with a 74-68 win in Waco. Ironically, beating Texas Tech in our final home game merely set the stage for a rematch three days later in the first round of the Big 12 tournament in Dallas. We lost 68-65 in a game we could have just as easily won.

I didn't know it at the time, but those two games against Texas Tech would be my final victory and loss as a head coach at the NCAA Division I level.

Both against Bob Knight.

The man who taught me everything.

However, Bob Knight didn't teach me about what I was about to do next.

The Financial Aid office continued to hound me through the spring, and I had a decision to make.

1. Would I get someone else to make the tuition payments (which was illegal)?
2. Would I confess everything and take my punishment for my bad decision?
3. Or would I make the payments myself (which was also illegal)?

No. 1 was out because, although I had great support from our booster group, I could never have asked them to do something illegal—no one had ever offered to help us illegally, nor did I ever ask anyone to help me "under the table." It would have disappointed our boosters tremendously. They were so excited about what we were accomplishing. Plus, I didn't want anyone else to know about what a mess I had made.

No. 2 was what I should have done, and I should have done it immediately at the start of school. I obviously would have faced repercussions, but it would have been a first-time offense for me, and the punishment would have been a great deal less than what transpired. But again, it came back to my pride. By the time I realized how impossible my task of raising the tuition money was, I didn't want anyone to know what a dumb move I had made by signing too many players. Prideful people don't admit their faults. They hide them.

So I decided on No. 3., to make the payments myself.

In other words, I cheated.

I made some small money order payments a couple of weeks before the end of school to appease the Financial Aid office. Gradually, I made more regular payments for both players, until, by the last day of the spring semester, I had completely paid off their debts.

I used funds from my personal summer camp account because I didn't want Claudia to know. Claudia had always been in charge of our checkbook, and we were always open about financial matters. Over all the years, she had been the consummate coach's wife. She was supportive of me while still keeping me grounded with her wise suggestions and being the greatest mother to our kids. Without her, I never would have had the success I had on the basketball floor. And yet, here I was, violating her trust by going behind the back of my very own wife.

By the last day of school, I had spent $40,000 of our money. I can't tell you how many times I asked myself what I was doing, but, at that point, I felt like there was no turning back. I had to keep up the charade.

I didn't even tell Doug Ash, who had been my loyal assistant for twenty-eight years. But this was precisely how secret my attempt at cheating was. I hid my actions from the two people who knew me best.

I must admit that when I made the final payments on the last day of school, I felt immense relief. I knew what I had done was wrong. But I also thought I got away with it. I had extinguished the fire that had raged for the previous seven months.

I was free in my mind.

But I was very guilty in my heart.

12

REVELATION

. . . Then she (Bathsheba) went back home. The woman conceived and sent word to David, saying, "I am pregnant."

2 Samuel 11:4b-5 (NIV)

In author Tom Wolfe's novel, *The Bonfire of the Vanities*, the reader watches protagonist Sherman McCoy's life spin painfully out of control. Essentially, this happens because of his pride. He is the master of his own universe. He makes a million dollars a year on Wall Street. He has a weekend house in the Hamptons. He has a family—a wife and a six-year-old daughter—but those relationships are shallow. He disguises his family and personal life with elegant living.

It's easy to see that his pride has already made him a reckless being. Eventually, his internal sin of pride leads to sinful actions. He has an affair with a woman named Maria; then he and Maria have an encounter in the Bronx with two men—an accident that leaves one of the men dead. He and Maria decide not to tell anyone about the incident. Sherman's pride not only leads to his wrongdoing but also prevents him from admitting his wrongdoing.

Sherman's life implodes. He ends up getting indicted for the crime, and, though he and his lawyer weasel their way out of the situation, all the legal issues turn his life into a seemingly eter-

95

nal headache. He experiences financial struggles, and his wife and daughter leave him.

Sherman McCoy wasn't the "Master of the Universe" he thought he was, after all. His pride caused him to do very foolish things; the consequences caused him to run and hide, lie and cheat, and in the end, his pride only left him paralyzed.

Very subtly, I, too, had become the master of my own universe, just like Sherman McCoy.

And my pride was apparently festering within as I attempted to maintain my "coaching reputation."

As my pride grew, and I became more and more competitive, I made compromises in my decisions. I didn't necessarily think everyone was cheating, but I did tell myself that everyone was probably "living in the gray area." And similar to the other David, I was so trusted at Baylor because of my past successes and clean record that I was essentially unaccountable for my actions. I would make the decision based on what was best for *me* and *my* Baylor basketball program and then make it fit into reality.

It's why I tried to downplay the large sum of money Dennehy and Herring owed and said to myself, "I'll figure it out." It's why I wasn't transparent with anyone when I couldn't figure it out. And it's why I paid for the scholarships without Claudia's knowing. This was *my* program, and *I* decided what was best.

The truth is, as I think back, I didn't even recognize myself anymore. I had become "desensitized" by my striving ambition. The only thing that seemed to matter was getting great players and winning games. It was as if I constantly had to "feed the dragon" that never got full.

In an attempt to be the best coach I could possibly be, I apparently set myself up as some kind of counterfeit CEO. I would make all the decisions because I knew what was best and, slowly but surely, the moth (me) kept flying closer to the flame. I may have given God a little credit for some of the great gifts and opportunities, but it was mostly about what I had done with the gifts. I considered my success to be pretty good because I had kept my coaching job for twenty-eight years, just like Sherman McCoy considered himself pretty good because of the millions he made on Wall Street.

Or you could just as easily insert King David of the Bible for Sherman McCoy. David lusted upon Bathsheba while she was bathing, sent his messengers to get her, slept with her, only to find out later she was pregnant with his child. At several points, he could have taken a step back and turned things around. Instead, his pride turned into a single sin, and his single sin turned into a multitude of sins, and his consequences became more severe.

And it didn't stop there.

It was a beautiful, hot Sunday afternoon in Texas during the summer of 2003, and my family and I were enjoying a long weekend at Horseshoe Bay in central Texas. This was several months after I made the last tuition payments for Patrick Dennehy and Cory Herring.

My phone rang.

It was Doug Ash.

"Hey, Doug," I said.

"Hey, Coach," he replied.

We had just completed a couple weeks of Baylor basketball camp, and Doug was just checking in with me, as he normally did at this time of year. At this point in the offseason, we were sorting through summer school arrangements, and Doug was calling all our players who were enrolled in summer school. Doug was the best at staying in touch with players in the offseason, especially the ones who needed it.

"Have you heard from Patrick Dennehy?" he asked. "I've been trying to get a hold of him for summer school, and I haven't heard back from him."

"No," I replied. "No, I haven't."

Doug and I agreed to meet the next morning to discuss summer school candidates and map out our summer recruiting period that was to begin in several days.

The fact that we went all of Monday without any sign of Patrick's whereabouts concerned me a little. At the same time, we weren't able to find Carlton Dotson either. They were good friends, and, since it was summer, we were thinking that they might be together somewhere. They might have just gone to visit some friends.

What I did find strange was that they hadn't contacted anyone else, either. Sunday, June 15, had been Father's Day, and yet neither of them contacted their parents. In the age of cell phones, it was truly bizarre to go multiple days without contacting a single person.

But then Tuesday passed. Then Wednesday.

And I began to wonder what was going on.

Soon after, a "missing person" report was filed, and the local media in Waco began to cover their absence. It was soon discovered that no one had heard from either of them since June 11. A few more days went by, and the stories in the media continued to pick up steam. Law enforcement officers interviewed me since I was the players' coach. I told them all I could, but obviously, I knew very little.

A few days later, we still did not have any answers, and I was now starting to grow very concerned. Later that week, it was reported that Carlton had been seen in Maryland. And by Thursday, authorities discovered Patrick's abandoned Chevrolet Tahoe in a parking lot in Virginia with both its license plates missing.

That's when I started thinking something might be horribly, horribly wrong.

Carlton's life had fallen apart at the end of his one season at Baylor. Although he had done exactly what we recruited him to do basketball-wise, his life away from basketball was anything but tranquil.

Before he transferred from Paris Junior College to Baylor, he had married a young lady he had known for a while, but the relationship didn't work out so they eventually got divorced. We had also revoked Carlton's scholarship due to a couple of disciplinary issues. It had to have been a difficult season for Carlton, and I felt terrible for him, but we gave him plenty of chances. (The media later made us out to be a drug-infested program, but the truth was we had only a couple of negative tests in four years. We found that interval-testing really helped get the point across.)

Patrick, meanwhile, had also been going through his own difficulties. Not only did he have to sit out the previous season because of the transfer rule, but he also blew out his knee in the first practice the previous fall, sidelining him for the entire year. His injury, I believe, led to a lot of dangerous down time for him. Instead of being involved with his teammates every day, he had to go to rehab for his knee. I believe this kept him from really feeling part of the team.

When Patrick's car was found in Virginia, the news went from a local story to a national story. Everyone in the country was suddenly talking about Baylor University—and for all the wrong reasons. I remember calling the coaches into my office and telling them, "I'm afraid we have something very serious on our hands."

There were detectives and authorities all over Waco. Lie detector tests were administered to some of the coaches and players. They were attempting to find out what people might know about the whereabouts of Carlton Dotson.

Mass hysteria was occurring at Baylor University.

Phones constantly ringing.

Theories flying.

Rumors spreading.

Families grieving.

Friends and teammates of Carlton and Patrick were all confused, and I was just as bewildered. To this day, the summer of 2003 is a blur to me. Had any coach in the history of college basketball dealt with something like this before?

I was also beginning to panic on a personal level. Obviously, I was concerned about their whereabouts, but I also began to panic out of selfish concerns. What if people started looking into Patrick's arrival at Baylor more closely? What if they examined his "walk-on" status? Things were happening so quickly that I couldn't keep up, and it became very apparent that the question surrounding the payment of Patrick's scholarship would eventually have to be answered.

When would I wake up from the nightmare?

On June 30, five days after authorities found Patrick's car, it was revealed that Carlton had told his cousin that he shot Patrick in the head over an argument while firing guns in rural Waco. There had been rampant speculation regarding all that might have happened, but this revelation shook the community. Could it be true? A teammate killing another teammate? And not just a teammate, but his friend? Theories abounded. Was it over drugs? Did it involve Carlton's ex-wife?

With each day that passed, there was a new discovery. For the first time in my coaching career, I was scared out of my mind. I could hardly process my thoughts. I was grieving for Patrick, and even Carlton, but, selfishly, I was also distressed about my impending doom. Although I had lied about the payments before, this compelled me to lie even more.

On July 21, it was confirmed: Carlton Dotson was going to be charged with murder. Four days later, Patrick was confirmed dead when they found his body in thick weeds near some gravel pits just outside Waco. He died of two gunshot wounds to the head.

I did not even know what to feel. My heart was broken over Patrick, and my tears that were photographed at his funeral were not an act. I couldn't help but think about how much promise he had, both as a person and as a player. I could hardly comprehend what was transpiring because of the magnitude of the tragedy.

13

URIAH

So David sent this word to Joab: "Send me Uriah the Hittite." And Joab sent him to David. When Uriah came to him, David asked him how Joab was, how the soldiers were and how the war was going. Then David said to Uriah, "Go down to your house and wash your feet." So Uriah left the palace, and a gift from the king was sent after him. But Uriah slept at the entrance to the palace with all his master's servants and did not go down to his house.

David was told, "Uriah did not go home." So he asked Uriah, "Haven't you just come from a military campaign? Why didn't you go home?"

Uriah said to David, "The ark and Israel and Judah are staying in tents, and my commander Joab and my lord's men are camped in the open country. How could I go to my house to eat and drink and make love to my wife? As surely as you live, I will not do such a thing!"

Then David said to him, "Stay here one more day, and tomorrow I will send you back." So Uriah remained in Jerusalem that day and the next. At David's invitation, he ate and drank with him, and David made him drunk. But in the evening Uriah went out to sleep on his mat among his master's servants; he did not go home.

2 Samuel 11:6-13 (NIV)

The same day they discovered Patrick's body, Baylor announced that three of its Law School professors were going to investigate the Baylor basketball program, specifically Patrick's situation. I knew this would mean trouble. Everything I had built in my twenty-eight years of coaching seemed to be on the cusp of crumbling. Although I think people's perceptions of me had generally always been somewhat positive, my sin of paying the tuition for two players was about to be revealed.

One of the three lawyers on Baylor's investigation team was a man named Bill Underwood. The fact that he was on the investigation was especially unsettling for me.

First of all, when I had arrived at Baylor, there were several faculty members who liked basketball and became good friends of mine. Professor Underwood and his fellow law professors were among them. He took special interest in the rebuilding of our program. I appreciated his support and passion for the program, but even more, I appreciated his friendship.

Second, Professor Underwood was also connected to my family because he was our son Robert's professor. Under a man like Professor Underwood at a school like Baylor, I knew Robert was going to get a remarkable education.

Third, he was known as one of the toughest professors at Baylor because he was so thorough. I knew this would work against me. Would one of my best friends at Baylor be the one to discover my payments?

I saw only one way out: I would have to lie my way out of the situation if I was to escape, and I would have to be lucky. This was making my situation even worse—I had to start lying to my friends and family. I was becoming so desperate that I was lying to everyone—even my athletic director, Tom Stanton, and University Counsel Noley Bice.

"Dave," Bill asked me in one of our first meetings, "you didn't pay for Patrick's scholarship, did you?"

He asked it casually, like a friend would.

I looked down for a second and then said, "No, Bill, I didn't."

But it didn't stop there. I not only lied, but I asked others to lie, also.

At one point, I flew up to Buffalo and met with Corey Herring's parents. I asked his parents to also lie to investigators. Before I went, I even called the Financial Aid office and posed as Corey's father, hoping to discover what types of questions they might ask his parents—an act of a desperate man.

Like King David, who was trying to encourage Uriah to sleep with Bathsheba, in order to take away his responsibility from the pregnancy, I was also trying to do everything I could to find a way out of the situation. I was micromanaging everything.

The only thing I couldn't do was tell the truth . . . or wake up from the nightmare.

In the morning David wrote a letter to Joab and sent it with Uriah. In it he wrote, "Put Uriah out in front where the fighting is fiercest. Then withdraw from him so he will be struck down and die."

So while Joab had the city under siege, he put Uriah at a place where he knew the strongest defenders were. When the men of the city came out and fought against Joab, some of the men in David's army fell; moreover, Uriah the Hittite died.

2 Samuel 11:14-17 (NIV)

Rumors about Dotson's failed drug test earlier that year began to surface. Consequently, there were some theories from the investigating team that perhaps Dennehy had paid for his scholarship through some involvement with the drugs. When Professor Underwood told me that they were pursuing that angle, I thought I might be off the hook. And that's when I had an idea: I would adopt their theory as my own. It was like a life preserver thrown in my direction. They were going to pursue that angle, and I would help them believe it. I grabbed on to this story out of desperation. I clung to it.

In other words, I would metaphorically send Uriah the Hittite to the frontlines of the battlefield in an attempt to cover my sins. Desperate people do desperate things. And I decided I would do everything I possibly could to protect all I had built. I was frantic. I had lost all sense of right and wrong.

I quickly went to work trying to do everything I could to give investigators reason to believe their own theory.

After the murder had been revealed, I had talked to some of the players who were still on campus getting ready for summer school. After the players had been given complete immunity, a few of the conversations revealed mention of some drug improprieties involving Dennehy and Dotson. Armed with this knowledge, as well as the information from the investigative team, I went to work trying match up the two groups.

I knew what the investigative team was looking for and heard what the players were telling me, so I got one of our coaches to get the players together. I took the players' stories and tried to organize them by giving them "talking points" and a tape recorder to practice. I was hoping that when the players told the investigators what they had told me, the investigators would no longer pursue the tuition payments and I might escape.

As wrong as this was, I wasn't thinking about anything other than saving my skin and my twenty-eight-year coaching career. Desperate people don't think clearly, and I was still hoping I would wake up from the nightmare that my life had become. Could this new theory of the investigators be my salvation?

Earlier that spring, Doug and I had hired a new, part-time coach to help our program. His name was Abar Rouse. Abar had been an assistant at the local junior college, and Doug and I had been impressed every time we had been around him. We hired him in place of one of our part-time assistants who had just stepped down, and he had done a very good job on his first assignment, helping with our June basketball camp.

Abar was a Baylor graduate and a twenty-seven-year-old kid who was eager to learn. We really liked Abar, but once everything started collapsing merely weeks into his new coaching job, I'm not sure if he knew what to think. This uneasiness in a strange surrounding, I think, is what caused Abar to start taping some of the conversations he was involved in.

Abar did not know who to trust.

"Sorry to keep asking you this," Bill said to me one day in a conference room at the Administrative Offices. "You swear you had nothing to do with Patrick Dennehy's scholarship?"

"No, I didn't, Bill," I told him as I looked away. I just could not look him square in the eye.

All during this period Claudia had no idea what I was up to. I even had to start lying to her, and what made it even worse is that she would pass the lies on to people who were concerned for us.

I obviously didn't consult her when I decided to keep the players that previous September; I obviously didn't consult her when I decided to pay for their tuitions on my own; and I obviously didn't consult her in the heat of the scandal. She was the most honest person I ever knew, but that's how bad things had become. Once you start lying you have to lie about everything, but lying to her bothered me the most.

I allowed a little sin to turn my life into something I never imagined. My series of lies had created someone I didn't recognize.

14

CONFRONTATION

The Lord sent Nathan to David. When he came to him, he said, "There were two men in a certain town, one rich and the other poor. The rich man had a very large number of sheep and cattle, but the poor man had nothing except one little ewe lamb he had bought. He raised it, and it grew up with him and his children. It shared his food, drank from his cup and even slept in his arms. It was like a daughter to him. Now a traveler came to the rich man, but the rich man refrained from taking one of his own sheep or cattle to prepare a meal for the traveler who had come to him. Instead, he took the ewe lamb that belonged to the poor man and prepared it for the one who had come to him."

David burned with anger against the man and said to Nathan, "As surely as the Lord lives, the man who did this must die! He must pay for that lamb four times over, because he did such a thing and had no pity."

Then Nathan said to David, "You are the man!"

2 Samuel 12:1-7a (NIV)

In the wake of David's affair with Bathsheba and the murder of her husband Uriah, God sends Nathan to confront David. The fact that God had to send Nathan alone reveals a lot about David's spiritual unconsciousness. Throughout his sin and cover-up, David failed to comprehend his rebellion against God, which meant that he sinned without repentance. And not only that, but David failed to see that the rich man in Nathan's parable was indeed himself!

This is what ambitious and powerful people do. They are so driven that their ignorance/forgetfulness of God's love also makes them ignorant of their sin. This was King David. This was also me, unfortunately.

In this phase of King David's life, he was ignorant of God's love, which led to his sin; his continued ignorance led to a massive cover-up that involved a murder; and his continued ignorance led to a spiritual unconsciousness that blinded him from all the crimes he committed—or else the Lord never would have had to send Nathan. Several times along the way, David could have stepped back and examined his life and actions. But self-examination is absent in a world that revolves around you because in that world, you aren't ever wrong. So why would you ever self-examine your actions and motives? People have placed you on a pedestal, and you kind of like it there.

I knew that time was not on my side. The more time that passed, the more clues they would gather—and all the arrows would point to me. Since I did not originally plan on paying for the scholarships, the way I went about paying for them was pretty sloppy for an Ivy League graduate. The arrows may as well have been neon signs.

The campus investigation got to the point where I was almost quarantined. Doug Ash was prohibited from talking to me; for the first time in twenty-eight years, he was no longer part of my life on a daily basis. This was another clue that they were starting to suspect I had paid the scholarships. I also noticed that when they questioned me, they were starting to be more and more business-like and skeptical in their approach.

After returning from Patrick's funeral, I had a message on my answering machine requesting that I meet with the investigative team the next morning. While these meetings were expected, when I walked into the conference room the next morning, I could tell the mood was vastly different.

All the lawyers on the investigation team were present. They looked up at me from the conference table as I opened the door and walked in. They did not seem angry, but I knew there was something different.

"Good morning, Coach," Professor Underwood said coldly.

"Good morning," I murmured, and I sat down.

Professor Underwood gave me a packet documenting all of my credit card transactions from the last month and all of the calls I made on my cell phone.

"Coach," Bill said, "I would like permission to look at your bank statements from the last year."

I looked at Bill, and then looked down at the table. I knew it was over.

This is what the Lord, the God of Israel, says: "I anointed you king over Israel, and I delivered you from the hand of Saul. I gave your master's house to you, and your master's wives into your arms. I gave you all Israel and Judah. And if all this had been too little, I would have given you even more. Why did you despise the word of the Lord by doing what is evil in his eyes?"

2 Samuel 12:7b-9a (NIV)

"May I talk to Professor Underwood alone?" I said softly. I don't know why I chose just to confess to him, but perhaps it was my way of finally showing him some respect.

All I heard were the squeaks of their chairs and the shuffling of their papers as the other members of the investigative team made their way toward the door. There were several pairs of eyes on me. But I sat in a daze, looking at my hands clasped together on the table.

I finally looked up at Professor Underwood, and it was as if I could finally see my life for what it had become. The charade was over. For the first time in a long time, I looked him right in the eye.

"I want to tell you about everything I have done," I started.

For the first time in months, I told him the truth.

After giving him an overview of my transgressions, Professor Underwood and I then walked across the quadrangle to President Sloan's office, where Tom Stanton met us with Noley Bice. There they were, four of my best supporters at Baylor, and I was going to tell them things that would cause them misery over the next few years. I knew everyone had to be upset at me, but they did not express their anger. I could tell they were disappointed by the way they looked at me. I felt as if they were saying, "I thought we were friends, Dave." It was decided I would resign immediately and that there would be a press conference at 5 p.m. that evening. The remainder of the day was terrible.

I stood in front of the media that evening and couldn't help but think of how I stood in front of them four years prior and answered questions about rebuilding Baylor's program. Back then, I had felt excitement in the room. Now I felt dismay. Then, Baylor Nation had welcomed me with open arms. Now, they were in shock. Then, I had shook hands all the way to my car in the parking lot. Now, I walked to my car alone knowing that everything I had just said would soon be all over *SportsCenter.*

And then I had to drive home and tell the woman that I loved how I had destroyed our life.

15

WHIRLWIND

This is what the Lord says: "Out of your own household
I am going to bring calamity on you."

2 Samuel 12:11a (NIV)

Whereas, I used to be perceived as somewhat of a "program builder" who revamped basketball teams, now I saw "disgraced" next to my name in the newspaper and "Fall From Grace" in every headline.

It was also my first time in nearly three decades that I wasn't a coach and did not have a job. This was torturous for me. For several days, Claudia would look at me as if she had no idea what I had become. And I knew there was truth in her look because I didn't know me, either. For the first time in our two-plus decades of marriage, I began to wonder if we would last. I knew she deserved better. She deserved a husband that was honest with her and led her in the right direction. I had lied to the most honest person I knew. I had lied to the very person I loved the most.

And my three children—what had I done to them?

Several days passed. Now out of work, my knee-jerk reaction was to go look for another job. So one day, I drove south on I-35 to talk with a friend about a position at a private school. I felt like it went fairly well, and then I drove back home. On my ninety-minute drive home, about halfway into my trip, my cell phone rang.

It was Mike Jones, the basketball reporter from the *Fort Worth Star-Telegram*.

Mike and I had become good friends over the years. Although some coaches had difficulties with members of the media, I had always made an attempt to get along with them because I always figured that we needed their help. I would go have a beer with some of them after the game, and by the end of the evening, I would have our ten-point loss down to a two-point loss. I really enjoyed their company. Even when they asked me difficult questions that annoyed me or seemed foolish, I respected the job they had to do. Mike and I always had a great relationship. I trusted him.

I answered my phone.

"Hey, Dave," he said in a guarded monotone. There was hesitation in his voice, as if he felt sorry for bothering me after everything that had unfolded.

"Look, I'm really sorry I have to do this," he explained. "This is not what I enjoy about this job. But your assistant coach, Abar Rouse, has given the *Star-Telegram* recordings of you attempting to cover up the payments. As a journalist, I have to ask you for a comment."

I don't even remember what I told Mike. As I finished the call, I was absolutely stunned. The fallout seemed to be expanding exponentially, and I had no idea what to do next.

The tapes damned me. Check that: my cover-up damned me.

Believe it or not, during the days after my resignation, I had a number of coaches call to encourage me, and about half of them admitted that they might have made the tuition payments, too, if they were in my position. They felt like the "5/8 Rule" was unfair to college programs across the country and understood that I had been in a difficult predicament.

Once the tapes were released, however, I became the biggest ogre in the sporting world.

Some people told me that Abar's lawyer had a vendetta against

Baylor president Robert Sloan, and I think she immediately saw an opportunity to hurt Dr. Sloan by releasing the tapes. Duke University head coach Mike Krzyzewski and Syracuse head coach Jim Boeheim later commented on the situation and said that an assistant who secretly recorded team meetings would never have a job on their coaching staffs—but more than anything, I knew none of this was Abar's fault. It was my entire fault. No one ruined my life. I ruined my life.

The transcripts were ugly—littered with lies and the locker room f-words—illustrations of a desperate man who would do anything to salvage his reputation. To the general public, I went from being a coach who resigned because he made a mistake to a sleazy manipulator who was trying to leverage someone's death in a scheme to save his career. Once again I became the center of another national media storm.

The press trucks rolled back in, and a couple of them parked in front of our house. They even tried to ask my wife questions when she walked out the front door. One of our "friends" in Waco saw Claudia one day and said to her, "When you've lost your reputation, you've lost everything." Claudia hadn't done a thing, and this lady hurt her badly.

As I fell, I took everyone I loved—my family, my friends, and my school, probably the 1,000 people closest to me—down with me. I felt like my actions disgraced an entire city and my family name. Who could ever have guessed that a selfish decision to illegally keep two basketball players would cause such fallout? If I would have known that all my lies and deception would destroy the very people I loved, I'm sure I would have acted differently. But prideful people struggle to think outside themselves; and consequently, the fallout of their sins hurts everyone.

Just like King David's cover-up, my cover-up also took things to an entirely different level. Both of our sins were exposed in broad daylight—his before all of Israel, mine before all of America. The balloon had popped, but the echo would not stop ringing in my ears. And this echo sent sound waves traveling across the country, and suddenly, my name was attached to one of the greatest scandals in the history of sports.

16

FREE FALL

Then David said to Nathan, "I have sinned against the Lord."

Nathan replied, "The Lord has taken away your sin. You are not going to die. But because by doing this you have shown utter contempt for the Lord, the son born to you will die."

After Nathan had gone home, the Lord struck the child that Uriah's wife had borne to David, and he became ill. David pleaded with God for the child. He fasted and spent the nights lying in sackcloth on the ground. The elders of his household stood beside him to get him up from the ground, but he refused, and he would not eat any food with them.

On the seventh day the child died.

2 Samuel 12:13-18a (NIV)

I couldn't believe what my life had become.

Several weeks after the tapes were released, I moved my family from Waco, Texas to Lakewood, Colorado (a suburb of Denver) because of the untenable firestorm that had developed over the incident. Our older son, Robert, valiantly remained at Baylor for his third year of Law School, and our daughter, Berkeley, returned to College Station for her junior year at Texas A&M. But Claudia (my wife), Jeff (our youngest child), and I all escaped to Colorado.

I was on the run, fleeing, doing whatever I could to escape the nightmare I was living, doing whatever I could to stop the free fall. I had felt compelled to move my family out of Texas because I thought a fresh start might work. I thought Colorado might be my safe haven. But there was no place I could run to escape the specter of my actions.

My family was still with me, but in my heart I knew I had disappointed them so much that it caused me to go through each day as a virtual zombie, existing without purpose, and hardly ever able to sleep. When my family would try to talk to me, I was oblivious to what they were saying. My mind was elsewhere, locked in a state of complete shock.

I was no longer Dave Bliss. I was something else.

Looking back on the move to Colorado, I realize that this decision couldn't have been worse and was just a continuation of a series of selfish choices I had recently been making. I should have left Texas by myself and allowed Jeff and Claudia to remain in Texas with Robert and Berkeley, where all their friends were. Truth was I had no idea how bad things were going to get or I never would have put Claudia and Jeff through the move. Although Claudia still had many friends in the Denver area, she was too embarrassed to re-connect. And if I was convinced that we should move, I should have settled us in Colorado Springs—where Claudia's parents and her sister resided—so they could have softened the transition. Instead, probably because of basketball reasons, I located us in Lakewood where we really didn't know anyone.

My wife was completely crushed and mystified that I had been so dishonest in our relationship. And our three children, who once enjoyed a special lifestyle as coach's kids, were now embarrassed by their dad and the name he had given them. I was confused and heartbroken over what I had done to my wife, family, and all the people I loved at Baylor.

I actually felt like a prison escapee—wearing a hat when I went in public, watching my back at all times, avoiding all direct eye contact.

On the run.

Every day was a struggle to get through. I had been a social drinker most of my life, but now, in the evenings, I would drink anything to try and numb my heartache.

The world went on, but it no longer needed Dave Bliss.

When I moved our family to Colorado, I did not know what to do with myself. For the first time in thirty-plus years, I had idle time. For the first time in three decades, I was no longer a coach.

Sometimes, just to get out of the house, I would drive around Denver with no destination in mind. Once, I remember pulling off Interstate 25 in downtown near the Pepsi Center where the pro basketball Denver Nuggets played. As I pulled up to the corner to make a turn, the light changed to red, and my stop put me eye-to-eye with a homeless person who was begging on the street corner.

Before the scandal, I would always train myself to never lock eyes with beggars on the street. But I didn't do that this time. On this particular afternoon, as I handed him a $10 bill, I did something else. I looked directly into this homeless man's eyes, and all I could see was the hopelessness in his trance-like gaze. And I realized that was exactly what I looked like now—completely defeated. It felt like I was looking into a mirror.

After coaching basketball for thirty-six years at the NCAA Division I level, I felt as if I had fallen off a cliff and was suspended in a never-ending free fall. But, unfortunately, my family and Baylor fell, too.

I fell because of the foolish decisions I made. They fell because they were tied to me. I had been blessed with a beautiful family and a wonderful job and I dragged them all through hell.

I learned very quickly that moving to the mountains could distance me from the Waco media, but no amount of miles would ever heal what I was feeling in my conscience and soul.

Because it was impossible for me to sleep, I would wake up early and go downstairs to wait for the morning newspaper to be delivered. Winter had come early to Colorado, so I usually started shoveling snow out of our driveway while I was waiting. As soon as the newspaper hit the pavement, I would immediately stop shoveling, take the newspaper to the garage, and start reading it.

In the past, I derived a great deal of enjoyment getting up early to grab the newspaper in order to read about a great win, like the game vs. Kansas. Now, however, my intentions were different. Instead, I was scanning the news to see if there were any bad articles about me. If I found an article, I would reluctantly decide whether I should tell my family, so they weren't caught off guard by it. But, gradually, there were so many articles and stories that I started to hide them.

To this day, I feel uncomfortable around snow because it reminds me of that time in my life. I didn't always dislike snow; there was a time I found it beautiful. Growing up in the Northeast, I used to love a refreshing snowfall. And when Claudia and I were first married, we would oftentimes vacation to Colorado, and I would be overwhelmed by the majesty of a snowfall in the Rockies.

But after my transgressions at Baylor, the snow in Denver made me feel different, almost prison-like in its effect on my life.

Denver is too beautiful to be a prison, but that's what it was like.

In Colorado, I found myself with nothing to do but reflect on my actions and wonder how I had gotten that way. Why did I feel I had to cheat? What kind of thinking led me to lose my moral compass? I didn't used to be this way. What on earth had happened?

I was completely shattered with absolutely no hope of ever again doing what I loved most—coaching college basketball. I had been terribly disappointed about things several times in my life (mostly involving basketball), but now all that I knew was complete emptiness. The emptiness was accompanied by a feeling of tremendous embarrassment and remorse. And, worst of all by far, guilt. To tell you the truth, the only things that could have made it worse would have been if my wife and family had left me. Fortunately, that didn't happen. We held on . . . somehow. But I wouldn't have blamed them if they had left.

It is hard to imagine someone damaging his life and family as much as I did without committing a misdemeanor or felony. And while I didn't commit a major crime, I had betrayed the public trust. My actions reflected a complete lack of integrity, something I never thought would happen.

And as if that wasn't enough, I was having difficulty finding another job, which added to the despair. This caused Claudia to grow increasingly frustrated with my idleness. Some nights, I would even play online chess until the wee hours of the morning, simply to fill the void of competition in my life.

I couldn't help but think about how good our life had been. This phase of my life, however, was the exact opposite. After enjoying the steady, elevator ride to the top, I was now in a free fall with no end in sight. I went from being a respected and successful Division I college coach to applying for minimum-wage jobs.

My reputation was ruined. My coaching days were over. From 500 NCAA victories, to this . . . online chess and no job.

After applying for a number of various positions, I eventually ended up getting a sales job in golf retail at Gart's Sporting Goods, now Sports Authority.

I liked golf, so that helped make the job fun, but I missed the feeling that accomplishment had given me in the past. Therefore, I made up my mind to do the best job I could at Gart's, regardless of my plight. I was never late for work and never took a sick day. I tried to have the cleanest area in the sports department. I kept this job for six months until, during my evaluation, I was asked to consider being a store manager. I figured they were pleased with my effort. The job was great because it got me out of the house, but it also taught me a lot about humility.

I had been hired at Gart's in November, right after the scandal, and it was the first winter in twenty-eight years that I wasn't in the thick of basketball season as a head coach. One weekend, there was a college basketball invitational in Denver. One of the teams came into Gart's, and I could see the players talking amongst themselves and whispering as I stood in the golf section.

Eventually, one of them came up to me and asked the question, "Are you Dave Bliss?"

"Yes," I said. "I am."

I remember watching the NCAA tournament at my house in Colorado in March of 2004.

It was painful revisiting a life I once knew. I thought about Baylor basketball, and how this was supposed to be our year, the year we would "get over the hump."

The worst thing about the NCAA tournament, however, was that it was something my family had looked forward to every year. Some of our fondest memories came from the whole NCAA tournament experience. We loved Selection Sunday. We loved seeing which city we'd be going to. And we loved calling our relatives or friends in that area and telling them we'd be coming their way. I enjoyed the NCAA tournament with our teams and the fans, but I really enjoyed it with my family. We made it a big party.

Now, I was hardly able to watch, thinking of all the people whose lives I had changed—both family and friends.

And I kept falling.

As the Final Four approached, there also came a new wave of attention from the media. My name had been tossed around on television and in the newspapers throughout the entire season, but the Final Four seemed to stir things up again, much to my dismay.

Although many asked for an interview, there was only one reporter I chose to talk to, and that was ESPN's Andy Katz. Andy had been the beat writer for the *Albuquerque Journal* when I coached at New Mexico, and I had always had a great relationship with him. Therefore, I decided to give Andy an interview for the Final Four. I opened up and hoped he would sense my remorse and write a favorable story.

The story didn't accomplish what I thought it might. At the time, I felt a bit betrayed by Andy. I questioned whether I should have given him the interview.

But now, looking back, I realize that all Andy did was tell the truth.

Rob graduated from Baylor Law in May 2004, but I was not able to attend his graduation. In the wake of all that happened, my attendance would have become a tremendous distraction. I can't imagine what Rob experienced during his final year at Baylor, but I knew I couldn't ruin his graduation, too. When he was accepted into Baylor Law three years before, I assume he was proud of his last name. By the time he left, he probably wanted to change it.

The day that Claudia left for Rob's graduation in Waco was a very difficult day. I stood by the window long after she pulled out of the driveway, and I thought about how I couldn't attend one of the crowning accomplishments of our firstborn son's education. I thought about him walking across the stage, accepting his diploma, and me not being there to share the occasion with him.

I can't imagine all the difficult moments that our children endured because of my actions.

Whereas a coach's kids are usually proud of their dad, this had to be unbelievably embarrassing. How do you process the situation as a child? Did my sins at Baylor undo everything I had done to raise them? I realize that many parents make mistakes, but when it was as catastrophic as mine was, there was no telling what the long-term effects might be.

As bad as things were personally, things were about to get real bad professionally, too.

After never even talking to an NCAA official for thirty-five years, I had several meetings with them within a year. In May 2004, I had a brutal five-hour and forty-minute meeting with the NCAA in Dallas. And in April 2005, twenty months after the scandal, I finally received my hearing in Indianapolis.

The morning of the NCAA hearing in Indianapolis was exactly as it should be, rainy and dreary. The damp streets made it feel as if the sun hadn't been out in a week. I felt as if I hadn't seen the sun in two long years. It was strange being back in Indiana, too, where Coach Knight had taught me everything three decades prior.

As I walked into an oversized, paneled conference room, I felt thirty sets of eyes on me. Besides the NCAA Committee members and Enforcement Officers being present, Robert Sloan, Doug Ash, Rodney Belcher, and some Baylor compliance officers were all there. I was ready to get everything behind me—kind of like the little kid who wanted to get his spanking over with. I had been completely honest with the NCAA since my last meeting with Professor Underwood. I needed to move on. My depression was significant.

As I looked around the room, I couldn't help but think that this was not the way it was supposed to be, that it didn't have to be this way. This was not what I learned from Bob Knight. He was the most honest coach I had ever known, and no other coach was even in second place.

Truthfully, an NCAA investigation is about the most disgraceful thing a head coach can endure. When you dream of being a coach, you don't picture yourself walking into an interrogation chamber at the NCAA headquarters. This room was my gallows.

I sat down at the far end of the table, next to Doug and Rodney. The members of the Committee on Infractions were seated at the opposite end. The Baylor representatives were to my left, and the NCAA investigators were to my right. The investigators started first and presented their case against me. When they finished, they asked if I wanted to make a closing statement.

"Yes, sir, I would," I said quietly, standing up. "I'm really sorry for disgracing the profession of coaching," I said. "President Sloan, I'm sorry for all that has occurred to you and the school that I care a great deal about. To all of you on the committee, I'm sorry for wasting all of your time. None of this should ever have happened. I have really let you all down. Words can't express how ashamed and disappointed I am."

I went on for a while longer, choking up several times, and then sat down. Several other people talked, but I didn't hear what they said because I was so over-wrought. At the conclusion, President Sloan and Tom Stanton walked down to my end of the table and shook my hand. It was a sad moment, but I appreciated it.

Several weeks later, I received my punishment—a ten-year show-cause penalty from the NCAA, restricting me for the next decade, one of the worst punishments an NCAA Division I basketball coach had ever received. I expected it to be bad, but not that bad.

Since Rob was in Law School when everything unfolded and Berkeley was in undergrad at Texas A&M, they kind of disappeared into their own worlds. I was in such extreme shock that I had no idea what to say to them or anyone. Although I couldn't see all the heartache that Rob and Berkeley were going through, I could with Jeff, who still lived with us since he was in high school.

Just as basketball was stripped from my life, I believe it was also stripped from Jeff's. I could tell early on that Jeff had a chance to be a basketball player. Rob and Berkeley had other interests, so I would do other things with them, but Jeff loved basketball the most of all of them. Growing up, he would wear his Michael Jordan jersey everywhere, even to church. He was a tow-headed basketball junkie.

He wasn't a great player as a freshman, but by the time he was a sophomore he had really worked on getting stronger and quicker and I started believing he could be a Division I player—certainly at a developing program like Baylor. A few days before my resignation, he told me he wanted to play for me at Baylor. And whereas I was happy on one hand, I also was paranoid of what was about to happen in Waco. That took a lot of the joy out of the occasion, which was never regained.

When I moved everyone to Colorado, we put him in Green Mountain High School, where a good friend of mine, Bruce Dick, was the coach. In the first game of his senior year, he scored 44 points against a really good team. All coaches' kids can shoot, and Jeff was no exception. Plus, he was tough.

My soiled reputation, however, deprived him of enjoying the type of experience he should have enjoyed. Although Coach Dick and his family went out of their way to help Jeff and our entire family, I felt that my presence was more of a hindrance than anything.

Looking back, I probably would have helped my family more by leaving them in Waco because that's where their friends were. Claudia had many friends and Jeff could have stayed with his school buddies. In Colorado, I really do believe that the "Bliss" last name was a real distraction. Jeff had some good colleges recruiting him, but he wanted a Division I opportunity—that's all he had ever been around. He ended up attending the University of Arizona, but his basketball career was over, thanks to me.

It was around Christmas time in 2005 that Claudia, Jeff, and I decided to go on a vacation to New York City. Few things are more beautiful than New York City at Christmas. Jeff was now in college at the University of Arizona and, with basketball not working out as he had hoped, he was beginning to discover a new passion: film. We decided to vacation to New York so he could check out one of the best film schools in the country, NYU.

It had been nearly two and a half years since the scandal unfolded at Baylor. Jeff and I had never really discussed the fallout that transpired in Waco, probably because we knew the deep wounds we both had from it. But that Christmas in New York, I could tell he was really frustrated with his life.

This coincided with a period where I was experiencing extreme depression, too. I was coming face-to-face with my sin and the consequences of that sin. Nothing was going right. And I had begun to come to grips with the reality that things would never be the same again.

I remember sitting in our hotel room in New York City alone with Jeff, sensing his frustration with his individual situation. Claudia had gone out shopping, and it was just my son and me.

"Jeff," I told him. "I can't tell you how terrible I feel about how all of this has worked out."

Jeff didn't say anything.

"I know this is all my fault," I told him. "And it's not fair to you. My actions denied you the opportunity to play college basketball. I'm so sorry."

We went back and forth for a period of time, both airing our hurts. Then, I hugged him, and we both cried.

The same trip to New York, Claudia and I helped Jeff film a movie for his class at Arizona. We would often times be actors for his films, and he was making another one during our trip to New York.

The premise of the film was that I spotted a previous female acquaintance (Claudia) across the restaurant and renewed our relationship. The restaurant was in Little Italy, and we also shot some scenes in Central Park.

Looking back, what Jeff had scripted and filmed was what I so deeply wanted with Claudia—a chance to return to a previous time in our relationship, to be together again without this chasm of dishonesty and betrayal between us.

Throughout this period, Claudia had amazing strength, as she fought to keep the family together. But, even as I watched all she did with and for the kids, I realized that our relationship had suffered irreparable harm. And whereas before, I always had been the family leader, now she was the strength of our family. I'm sure there were a lot of times where she wanted to just get away from me and the horrible situation that I had created, but her love and compassion for her "brood" kept her from leaving.

"For better or worse" took on superhuman proportions during this time. I was so grateful that I had married a woman from such a solid, faith-based upbringing. Although divorce was certainly an option at this time, her dedication to her children outweighed her personal disappointment in me.

I was absolutely drained emotionally and, as a result, I was of absolutely no help to her. As I look back to this time, I wish I could have been stronger, either for Claudia or the kids, but such is the impact of my shame and embarrassment.

The media storm faded as more scandals in the sporting world had come and gone, but inside, I was dispirited, void of the hope of anything getting better.

And I kept falling.

17

BROKEN

Have mercy on me, O God,
according to your unfailing love;
according to your great compassion
blot out my transgressions.
Wash away all my iniquity
and cleanse me from my sin.

For I know my transgressions,
and my sin is always before me.
Against you, you only, have I sinned
and done what is evil in your sight;
so you are right in your verdict
and justified when you judge.
Surely I was sinful at birth,
sinful from the time my mother conceived me.
Yet you desired faithfulness even in the womb;
you taught me wisdom in that secret place.

Cleanse me with hyssop, and I will be clean;
wash me, and I will be whiter than snow.
Let me hear joy and gladness;
let the bones you have crushed rejoice.
Hide your face from my sins
and blot out all my iniquity.

Create in me a pure heart, O God,

and renew a steadfast spirit within me.
Do not cast me from your presence
or take your Holy Spirit from me.
Restore to me the joy of your salvation
and grant me a willing spirit, to sustain me.

Then I will teach transgressors your ways,
so that sinners will turn back to you.
Deliver me from the guilt of bloodshed, O God,
you who are God my Savior,
and my tongue will sing of your righteousness.
Open my lips, Lord,
and my mouth will declare your praise.
You do not delight in sacrifice, or I would bring it;
you do not take pleasure in burnt offerings.
My sacrifice, O God, is a broken spirit;
a broken and contrite heart
you, God, will not despise.

Psalm 51:1-17 (NIV)

I hit with a thud.

Rock bottom is exactly that.

King David wrote Psalm 51 shortly after Nathan confronted him about his affair with Bathsheba and his murder of Uriah. It's a psalm that pleads for forgiveness, reflects David's brokenness, and finally shows a consciousness of his sin and a desire to repent. It took at least three years for me to truly understand this psalm.

I understood that I was guilty of "showing utter contempt to the Lord," as Nathan tells David in 2 Samuel 12. The King James Version uses the word "blaspheme" instead of "utter contempt," and I did indeed understand that I had both blasphemed my Christian witness and shamed my family. I understood that both of those needed to be rectified. The problem was that I had absolutely no idea how to do it.

What I did not yet understand was the end of Psalm 51—that when there was nothing left for me to give, when Jesus was all I had, perhaps all the Father wanted from me was a "broken spirit" and a "broken and contrite heart." Maybe brokenness was the key.

Though the Tower of Babel I had constructed crumbled to the ground around me, I was also dispirited because of what was happening inside me. Just as I was on the run externally, by fleeing Texas, I was also lost internally.

Immediately following the scandal at Baylor, I remember someone telling me that I was a "good person who just happened to do a bad thing." It sounded better than some of the other things that were being said about me, so I adopted that as my mantra.

Though I felt horribly about what happened at Baylor, initially this was mostly out of the humiliation of being caught. And this was mostly because my entire identity and level of importance in this world had been wrapped up in being a successful basketball coach. I felt badly, mostly for selfish reasons. But I was not broken spiritually. I hadn't had time. I was still professing that I was a good person who had done a bad thing.

There is no doubt that this was a type of denial because there was no way a "good person" would have done any of the things I did.

Now, although my entire pretentious world had fallen apart, spiritually I remained just as ignorant and naive. Similar to David when he did not realize the character in Nathan's parable was himself, I was unfamiliar with "brokenness," so, consequently, I lived a life absent of repentance. I was lost spiritually.

Throughout my coaching life, I was always confident that there was some solution to help get me out of a hole. I could always solve my problems by "striving" harder. I could go back to the coaching laboratory and fix whatever was wrong. I was the eternal optimist—one who could always seem to be able to get the ship righted, no matter how bad the situation was. For some time after the scandal, this is what I tried to do in my own life. It was as if

I was trying to convince each person of my mantra that I was a "good person who had done a bad thing." I would tell one person, and then I was off to tell the next person. Those people had to really wonder what was going on.

And I tried the same thing with the media. That's why I agreed to do the Final Four interview with Andy Katz, for example—I was attempting to change people's minds in any manner I could because this is what I had done before. Explaining why I had my team in a zone defense was a great deal different, however, than justifying my actions at Baylor.

This works-based mindset applied to my spiritual life as well. Though God was certainly teaching me things during my free fall, I was also trying to prove to God that I was not a bad person, as if this newfound devotion to Him could somehow undo all I had done in His eyes.

But it all left me empty and hopeless. It was futile, as long as I thought I could do it myself. Something always seemed to remind me of my past sins.

I was terribly depressed, insecure, and desperate for something that could fix me from within. All my attempts at personal restoration had failed. I woke up every morning to the same depression—Groundhog Day in hell—with no hope and no direction. Although I had no experience at what a broken life was like, I came to realize that "broken" described my new life perfectly. Without any previous experience of this brokenness, I had no idea what to do.

It was obvious that I didn't need to change other people's minds; I needed to change mine!

While David's sin was a lust of flesh; mine was a lust of ambition, fame, and greed. Following his sin, David was faced with an unplanned pregnancy. Following mine, I was faced with an unplanned murder. David reacted with what Chuck Swindoll, in his book about David, calls a "panic cover up;" I also reacted with a "panic cover up." Very rarely are good decisions made when someone is in a panic-mode, and King David and I were no exceptions.

The sins and cover-ups King David and I committed resulted in further shame for both of us. It wasn't until Nathan confronted David that he was broken before the Lord; and it wasn't until I realized that I had absolutely hit rock bottom that I was broken before God. I remember hearing the expression, "When God is all you have, you'll find that God is all you need."

In studying David's genuine repentance in Psalm 51, I learned that he went through four stages:

1. His admission of guilt.
2. His complete break from sin.
3. His broken spirit.
4. His claiming of God's forgiveness and reinstatement.

At this point in my journey, I was at No. 3—absolutely broken, desperate for hope. All I had to offer to the Lord was a "broken spirit" and a "broken and contrite heart," as David says at the end of Psalm 51. God seemed to say to me, "Stop trying, David. Stop trying to fix everything! Just come to Me."

Maybe God wanted me to stop trying to fix myself and allow Him to fix me. Maybe He wanted me to stop working and allow Him to work *through* me.

Every time I looked in the mirror after the summer of 2003, I had real difficulty looking myself in the eye. All I saw was the face of a man who had been given so much but had squandered it all; the face of a man who, like King David, had been given a kingdom and a platform but had allowed it to be swept away by his striving spirit of ambition and pride.

At my lowest point, after I had hit rock bottom, I remember waking up in the middle of the night and going downstairs so I wouldn't wake Claudia. As I pressed my tear-stained face into a pillow, lying face down on the floor, I pleaded to God, "Father, please help me. I don't know how my life has gotten this messed up, but I'm so scared and don't know what to do. I don't see any hope, and I need your help. This is so complicated that only You can help fix it. Please help me. I'm so sorry for all I have done to my family and Baylor, and I am so lonely."

I was broken, in complete and utter despair—just like King David.

Little did I know, as similar as my actions were to King David's, I would soon awaken to another one of our similarities.

The meaning of the name we shared.

PART 3

BELOVED

18
AUTOPSY

The freefall following the scandal had left me in a heap, virtually lifeless, a completely broken man who had lost most of his hope. My family was struggling, my career was in ruins, and my life was in stagnant disarray.

For over thirty years I had chased the deceptive prize of success. A couple of times I thought I was going to get there, but then Baylor happened and, in a second, everything was gone. And not only gone, but in its place I had the smoldering ashes of a wasted career and a shattered life. I had strived for success, and it had been a big lie. As I surveyed what was left in the debris, I was even more concerned about the deterioration of my character.

And for the first time in my life, I had absolutely no solution for any of what was occurring in my life.

I had heard and read about people who told of being completely broken, spiritually and emotionally, but I never, ever thought it would happen to me. For fifty-nine years, my life bordered on the idyllic, but now, here I was—completely and thoroughly devastated. I had gone, much too truly, from the penthouse to the outhouse.

In the three years following the scandal, it finally became painfully obvious to me that I was incapable of restoring my own life. I was completely helpless and, although I may have thought of God as a Straitjacket Santa Claus before, now I needed a God of

Miracles.

Could He help me? Would He help me?

One morning, I had a flashback to several years before when we lived in New Mexico.

It was a beautiful Saturday morning in Albuquerque, and Claudia and I had decided that I would take our three kids and have a "Putt-Putt Morning." We had a basketball game later that evening at The Pit, so it was decided that I would take the kids out for breakfast, go play miniature golf, and finish with some arcade time. Normally this would occupy three hours or so, and it would also accomplish two rather important things.

One, taking the kids would give Claudia a break from the clamor of the week and, two, it would give me some "alone time" with my children. Coaching is a great profession, but because of the tunnel-vision approach you give to every phase of the job, quite often you might be present physically with your family but absent mentally. Each time we did this little outing, I would realize how fortunate we were to have such lovable and healthy children.

We set out a little after 8 a.m. and arrived at an IHOP several minutes later and were immediately seated. We were handed a large plastic menu that contained every egg and pancake combination possible. Ten-year-old Berkeley chose first and selected a "Happy Pancake" with its whipped cream smile. Jeff, who was five, wanted a waffle, and Robert, eleven, chose the chocolate pancakes that resembled a superhero. I ordered the short stack, with a scrambled egg, as a future exchange for any of their orders that didn't taste right. I was getting used to eating Happy Pancakes.

Next, it was off to miniature golf. The teams were decided on the ride over. Robert and Berkeley vs. Jeff and Dad, winners take all. Things were going pretty normal until the third hole, the dreaded "Windmill Hole," and Robert was up first. He putted his ball down the green carpet and through the rotating windmill; it hit the bank board on the other side and caromed to within six inches of the hole. He was ecstatic. His sister promptly did likewise—down the carpet, through the windmill, and off the bank board until the ball came to rest about a foot from the hole. She immediately received a high five from her brother.

Now it was little Jeff's turn, and I could tell something bad was about to happen when I saw him wind up, golf club high above his shoulders, for a herculean swing at his little green ball. Last I saw that ball, it had hit the top of the windmill, ricocheted off the clown's face on hole No. 6 to our left, and bounced over the fence, rolling down I-25 South toward El Paso. The two older kids were laughing and jumping up and down, but poor Jeff was devastated.

I attempted to tell him that everything would be okay, but before I could say a thing, he looked up at me, with tears rolling down both cheeks, and begged, "Daddy, can I have a do-over?"

And now, several years later and in my broken state, from my lowest ebb, lying prostrate on the floor, I begged God for my "do-over"—another chance at life.

For the next few months, not knowing what else to do, I would get up before sunrise, go quietly downstairs, and open my Bible. I had read parts of the Bible sporadically before, like the book of Luke at Christmas and the book of Matthew at Easter. Overall, most of my reading had been in the New Testament. Although I carried my Bible with me to church and when I went to speak for FCA or some Christian group, it was more of a prop because I was unfamiliar with what it contained.

I had never read much of the Old Testament because I would get bogged down in Leviticus and Numbers. But I felt like I should start at the beginning, so I did. After reading through Genesis, I slogged through Deuteronomy and read through the rest of the Old Testament—the historical books, poetry books, major prophets, and minor prophets. Then I made my way through the Gospels and Epistles in the New Testament, finishing with the Book of Revelation. For the first time in my life, I *really* read the Bible. All of it. Perhaps it was because I was so destitute, but the Bible seemed to be communicating to me in a brand new way. I did not always understand what I was reading, but for some reason, it seemed to help me. I began writing my thoughts down on a yellow legal pad that I had once used to prepare game plans. Maybe these thoughts were becoming my game plan now. I had never been a journal-type person before, but I became one. And pretty soon, I had not only filled up the legal pad, but several more notebooks, as well.

I would keep a journal for the next ten years.

I may have been learning a lot, but it was still an uneasy period for me. I had never been this run-down mentally before. Over the next six months, God performed an "autopsy" on my broken state. He threw me up on the table and started cutting. His brutal examination of Dave Bliss showed me several things I didn't like about myself, but most of all it revealed that all my striving had only served to complicate my life and lead me astray.

Striving, by itself, isn't bad when it involves working hard. But my striving seemed to be very self-serving—a "me, myself and I" striving—and it was as if I was willing to climb over anything and anybody that might keep me from being perceived as a success.

Basically, I could sense three basic components to God's evaluation: my prideful ambition, my human insecurities, and my lack of accountability. In concert, they all had exacted a toll by changing me into someone I didn't even recognize.

• **The first component—pride—revealed surprising character flaws of which I was completely unaware.** I had allowed the prideful world of competitive athletics to compromise my value system.

At every stop in my coaching career, I wanted to be thought of as someone who was a good coach, who could not only rebuild and ignite the excitement of success in a community and in a team, but who also played by the rules.

I now realized that I would be forever thought of as a cheater, but that hadn't been the case for most of my twenty-eight years as a head coach. With the exception of a brief period in the early 1980s when my SMU program got away from me during the "Ponygate" era of Mustang athletics, Doug and I prided ourselves on "doing it the right way." The SMU period was a result of a bad culture that existed in the Mustang athletic department during this time, and I was very disappointed that it occurred under my watch, but we got it corrected quickly.

Looking back, however, I wonder if this was the start of me blurring my lines between right and wrong.

It was now pretty obvious to me that my coaching talents were God's gift to me, but in my quest to attain basketball coaching fame, these talents had become all about me. When I had entered coaching thirty years before, I chose the profession because I enjoyed the opportunity of helping young people, but now, looking back, it became more about "using" the players to show the world what a great coach I was.

At each coaching stop, I worked even harder than the previous job. I was constantly looking for an edge—something that would enable our program to separate from the pack and allow me, the "coaching star," to shine even brighter. Whatever it took—making more calls, making more visits, watching more games, or studying more tape, I did them. Work, work, and work some more. We had succeeded before, and I was determined that we would do it again. It was a hunger that could not be satisfied, a dragon that had to be fed. But the predictable fatigue and impatience resulted in several bad decisions.

• **The second component was my basic insecurity as a human.** Although I never had a job where I felt my position as coach was in jeopardy, I discovered that I worried too much about what others thought about me. Instead of being secure in the knowledge that my career was under God's control, I allowed the applause of others to turn my head.

When I started coaching, I was making a four-figure salary; by the time I got to Baylor, I was making a six-figure salary. Sports in America, certainly because of television, spiraled upward in interest from the late 1960s to the 2000s. Coaching had changed; the old grizzled veteran in the gray sweatshirt with a whistle around his neck had been replaced by a newer, shinier model—coaches who worked the sidelines in fashionable suits and expensive loafers. Now coaches were looked at as being much more professional, especially winning ones, and the escalating salaries reflected this celebrity status. I never complained when they paid me more money, but it never seemed right that a coach should come even close to making what the president of the university made.

The result sometimes was that coaches were placed on a pedestal in their community and received all kinds of unwarranted adulation and praise. This attention had both good and bad sides to it, depending on how you let it affect you. It seemed that I had allowed this pedestal status to make me feel more important than was healthy. This is never a good position for a man to be in. Instead of fleeing when I was tempted to grasp beyond the acceptable boundaries, I gave in and cheated because I wanted more for myself.

My priorities were all wrong—I had pridefully sacrificed my important relationships to gain the approval of people I never knew, or had any real reason to respect or care about their opinion.

• **And lastly, I had allowed my past successes to desensitize me.** I felt whatever I did was right. The administration at Baylor had allowed me leeway in operating the Baylor basketball program, but I had abused it. The Bible's warnings about pride seemed to have come true in my own life:

> *Success breeds confidence.*
> *Confidence breeds entitlement.*
> *Entitlement breeds desensitization.*
> *Desensitization breeds invincibility.*
> *Invincibility breeds carelessness.*

And although God's autopsy seemed to reveal these serious

flaws, it also seemed like He was offering two life-giving antidotes.

- **I could put Jesus on the pedestal, rather than myself.** God proffered that, from this point forward in my life I would do well to put Jesus on the pedestal. And so, every morning, rather than worrying about what was going to happen to me that day, I thanked God for loving me enough to chasten me. The remainder of the day I tried to concentrate on things that I thought would reflect a faithful spirit, whether I was working at Gart's or mentoring a high school coach.

- **I could focus on serving the "Audience of One."** God also seemed to admonish me to stop worrying about trying to please the world. This time around, all I had to do was please Him. From this point forward, He would be my Audience of One.

I knew that it was not going to be that easy, I knew there was a caveat. The consequences for my actions had already begun, and I expected some very tough times ahead. But then I read that the wilderness wasn't meant to be permanent and if I was determined to change, I wouldn't go through it alone . . . God would be with me. Although there might not be any guarantees, I was determined not to quit.

Brokenness causes you to be tremendously vulnerable, a feeling from which most men cower. Slowly, however, I could sense that God seemed to be cracking through my shell of ignorance, arrogance, and pride. As uncomfortable as all this introspection was making me, I derived a small degree of comfort doing something that seemed to create some positiveness in my life.

I discovered through my brokenness that I definitely needed to change my ways. I also knew that now I was, indeed, completely dependent upon Him. That being said, it seems it shouldn't take something as catastrophic as I was experiencing to make anyone—any of us—realize our neediness. Our need for God is in our very nature as human beings. The Apostle Paul makes it as total, as comprehensive as he could in Romans 3:23 when he wrote that "all have sinned and fall short of the glory of God." Similarly, the Prophet Isaiah in Isaiah 64:6 (KJV) says that "we are all as an unclean thing, that all our righteousness are as filthy rags."

Man is fallen, and God is perfectly holy. Therefore, brokenness is bound to occur. And the feeling of "brokenness" isn't just reserved for someone whose world has crumbled, as mine did. "Brokenness" seems necessary for all of us and, as unlikely as it seemed, I was learning that sometimes "brokenness" could be a good thing. Author Brennan Manning, in his book *The Ragamuffin Gospel*, calls it having a "tilted halo" as opposed to a "tight halo." People with "tight halos" trust in their own works and their own efforts. These were the Pharisees in Jesus' day. Says Manning:

> *To be alive is to be broken. And to be broken is to stand in need of grace. Honesty keeps us in touch with our neediness and the truth that we are saved sinners. There is a beautiful transparency to honest disciples who never wear a false face and do not pretend to be anything but who they are.*

Bruised, battered, and beaten, I finally gave up.

I admitted defeat and from the despair of complete brokenness, I relinquished my clay to God.

19

CROSSROADS

My phone rang. It was from a Colorado Springs number I wasn't familiar with, so I didn't pick it up. When I listened to the voicemail, the person who called said his name was Gary Lydic. He seemed genuinely concerned about me, although I did not recognize the name immediately. Nevertheless, I decided to call him back.

"Hi, this is Dave Bliss," I said. "I'm returning your call."

"Hi, Dave," Gary said. "You probably don't remember me, but we've met before."

"Okay?" I said, cautiously curious.

"I've helped with the National Association of Basketball Coaches at the Final Four, and I work with Athletes in Action and the Fellowship of Christian Athletes in preparing programs for coaches and their wives at the tournament."

"That's nice," I replied, trying to connect all the dots.

Gary and I talked for a little longer, and he explained that he was working in the pastor outreach department at Focus on the Family in Colorado Springs, just an hour south of my home outside Denver. The ministry had been founded by Dr. James Dobson, who had a nationwide radio show. To this day, I don't know what prompted Gary to call, although he later told me that someone had suggested he might want to check on me.

As we ended our brief conversation, he invited me to come down to the Focus on the Family headquarters. I thanked him for calling, and told him—without much enthusiasm or, in truth, sincerity—that I would think about it.

The more I thought about Gary's proposal, however, the more I felt I should take him up on it. I was really struggling with my depression, and there was something about his sincerity that gave me comfort. Gary said he wasn't a counselor, but he said he would be glad to meet with me and just talk—as a friend. This sounded different, so a couple of days later I called Gary back and said I'd like to meet him. I figured I had nothing to lose.

At the spacious reception area at the Focus on the Family headquarters, I was greeted by a pleasant young lady. I told her I had an appointment with Gary Lydic, and moments later a well-dressed, healthy man in his fifties was coming down the stairs, sporting a broad smile. After a hearty handshake, he invited me to follow him back upstairs, where we entered a small conference room—your typical conference room, with a couple of couches and a pitcher of water on a table. I sat down, nervous, but something about Gary made me feel comfortable.

We small-talked about mutual friends, and then Gary looked directly at me and asked me how I was doing. Reflexively, I said I was okay, but then he began asking me more questions. Before I knew it, I was sharing parts of my story with Gary I hadn't shared with anyone. As I continued to talk with him, he seemed in as much anguish as I was, sharing my hurt.

As time went on, it became more and more apparent that Gary was exactly what I needed. He didn't just attempt to make me feel better; he was telling me truth that I needed to hear—biblical truth. Up to then, I really think most people were afraid of my story.

This period with Gary Lydic, however, was the start of trying to put the pieces back together.

As I look back, perhaps it was God who prompted him to call me out of the blue.

I continued meeting with Gary for the next few months, driving down to Colorado Springs five or six times. Each time we talked, he could tell how concerned I was for Claudia and Jeff. As a result, Gary was nice enough—intuitive enough, truly caring enough—to ask if he could drive up to Denver to watch several of Jeff's basketball games. Gary was a basketball nut and had played a lot of pick-up games with Dr. Dobson back in the day.

With each succeeding visit, I opened up more and more, as God used Gary to draw out the pain and guilt I was experiencing. I'm sure of that. As we were figuratively standing together over the ashes of my ruined career, he wouldn't *let* me think that all was lost.

Gary explained many things to me about man's sinful nature and God's provision for these flaws through His Son, Jesus Christ. He also challenged my thinking, questioning *why* I did certain things. He introduced the idea that perhaps my striving ambition to be a successful basketball coach had become my mistress—my "graven image" prohibited by one of the Ten Commandments. I had never thought about it like that, but the more I did, the more I believed he might be right. I had become consumed with coaching, and coaching success, at the expense of everything else that should have been important to me.

Each time I met with Gary, no matter what we had discussed that day, he always seemed to spark a perception of hope in me. A little surprised about it myself, I was thinking positively again. We discussed some very difficult issues, but I never left that conference room without feeling encouraged and motivated to keep battling.

Somehow, his "coming alongside me" worked wonders in my spirit, transcending despair. Maybe this was the way the Christian life was meant to be lived—in fellowship with encouraging friends.

A year or so after I began meeting with Gary Lydic, my "mistress" came knocking on my door again.

I was in Albuquerque in August 2005 when one of my assistants from New Mexico and Baylor, Brian Walsh, called and asked if I might be interested in coaching in the Continental Basketball Association (CBA) for the Dakota Wizards, a team in Bismarck, North Dakota. Brian had just resigned as coach because he felt he needed to stay closer to home.

Brian called the owner of the Dakota Wizards, and they were receptive to considering me. I flew up there and talked them into hiring me. The Wizards had a lot of local support, and I know their hiring me caused a bit of a stir in their basketball community. However, the Wizards owner and general manager were very supportive and did everything they could to make my stay successful.

With my hiring, the media of course got involved again. I saw it as another possible opportunity to tell people how I had "changed." This latest PR attempt included Andy Katz and his production team from ESPN, the *Fort Worth Star-Telegram*, the *Dallas Morning News*, and the *Minneapolis Tribune*. *Cold Pizza*, *CBS Evening News*, and HBO also called to do a show, but I felt like that was too much. Therefore, I declined every interview except those with writers I knew. The ensuing articles were okay, but I finally came to grips with the fact that I would never be able to explain my way back into the good graces of the world.

These became my last interviews for three years.

Because the Wizards played only two or three games a week, I had a lot of downtime, especially since Claudia remained in Denver and Jeff had gone off to college. Most days, I had plenty of time to dive into books like C.S. Lewis's *Mere Christianity* or A.W. Tozer's *The Purpose of Man*. The more I read, the more I learned; and the more I learned, the more I wrote in my journal.

Although I may have gone to Bismarck intending to get back involved with basketball, albeit at the professional level, that's not what happened. In late January, I remember waking up in the early hours with Matthew 6:33 ringing in my head: "But seek first his kingdom and his righteousness . . . "

Something about the verse stayed with me for the next few weeks. As I thought about things more and more, I reconsidered my decision to go back into coaching. I began to sense I was doing the same thing I had done before—"striving" after my career. Was I still trying to regain my coaching reputation, still working to prove my worth, still trying to tell people I was a "good person who did a bad thing"?

Please, read nothing negative about Bismarck into this. I loved my time there. The people were great to me, as were the players, and I got involved in a terrific Bible study. But it was apparent that I had too much of a learning curve in order to coach in the pro game. My sojourn to North Dakota served as an unintended eye-opener and more importantly, I now understood what my most important priority should be.

I resigned at the end of the season and drove back to Denver to be with my family.

I thought about the three decades I spent as a head coach at the Division I college level, and realized that, although the pages of my life kept turning through my many coaching opportunities, I had not taken the time to truly enjoy the Author of my book, to appreciate His primary role. I was missing out on the experience of discovering God and learning what He had truly created me for.

I felt that this was my inadvertent ignorance.

And, I was learning, one of the most dangerous things about that particular kind of ignorance, is it almost always leads to arrogance. Refusing to acknowledge God's loving influence working in your life—almost surely will—lead you to a type of arrogance about yourself. You start thinking that *you* are the reason behind all your success.

I knew all along that I owed my complete existence to God, but in a dismissive way, I hadn't given Him the respect commensurate with the gift. Always I felt He was "out there," but if I believed God to be so distant, how could I possibly see His involvement in my day-to-day actions?

If I had recognized His constant presence, I see absolutely no way that I would have committed the atrocious acts at Baylor. I would have honored Him by a humble acceptance of my role in coaching as an opportunity to serve God from the position in which He had led me, had placed me. Instead, I was so busy with my head down trying to climb *my* "ladder of success" that I did not take the time to look up and thank the Author. This was because I did not know the truth about the qualities of God. But how would I? I never ever really thought about the relationship, let alone trying to pursue it.

I now believe that each person must eventually answer questions regarding certain truths in his or her life.

Do I really believe in God?

What is He like?

Do I know who Jesus is?

Do I believe the Bible?

Will my life be about myself, or will it reflect something much greater? There is no middle ground. As I found out, partial obedience turned out to be disobedience. These faith-based decisions have to be at the very crux of every man's existence, a "crossroads" of sorts.

My period in North Dakota (too many "crossroads") made me question whether or not I wanted to stay in my rut and do the exact same things all over again. I decided it was time for a change. Time to break away from the old. Time for God to take charge. I looked back on my life and began to wonder: If the purpose of life is to truly glorify God and enjoy Him, had I ever been really living at all?

The Dakota Wizards coaching opportunity forced me to answer a number of questions: Would I return to my life as I knew it before, or would I finally repent and commit to God's purpose for my life? Would I continue to tacitly accept Jesus as my Savior or step into the unknown territory of making him Lord? Would I continue trying to write my own comeback story or finally surrender the pen?

And finally this: If I die to myself, would I finally live?

20

FULL SURRENDER

For most of my life, I felt somewhat respected for what I had accomplished in this world, but I knew that those days were over. It was apparent that there was nothing I could personally do to reclaim my reputation. It didn't matter how many hands I shook, or how many people I tried to tell, "I'm a good person who did a bad thing." There was no amount of good I could do to untangle the summer of 2003. Talking to the media couldn't change anything. Coaching in North Dakota couldn't change anything. And further striving would be futile.

In fact, I had come to feel that striving was the exact opposite of surrendering to God. Striving says, "I can and will do everything." I had finally found out that this was not true. And this discovery left me feeling depressed. If I could no longer strive, how would I ever know if I was a success?

It was becoming clearer, as I realized that I could not fix myself, that surrender was where I needed to be. My sin broke me and all appeared lost, but then I discovered that God was offering me a new alternative. He was asking me to trust Him—to surrender to Him and allow Him to be Lord of my life. He was convincing me that He could change me and still fulfill His purpose in my life.

Talk about a bad trade for Him—my deplorable, sinful existence for His offer of a life of peace. The decision for Full Surrender had never been clearer—how could I have missed this?

I grew up in a time when listening to the radio was large part of life, but sometimes—during storms, for example—there would be an irritating, crackling interference, which we called static. When all you heard was static, you usually tuned out. Before my fall, my communication with God was "staticky" at best. And most of the time, I was working so hard and going so fast through life, I apparently tuned Him out—but that wasn't His fault.

This "new surrender" was not an easy concept for me, and God conveyed that it would take more obedience and perseverance than I've ever required in anything before, but with His help, things started to change. And I started to feel some hope in my spirit again. I think God was aware I was making some progress in my recovery.

The world would have us believe that our success rests on our appearance and our performance because that's what is communicated on television and in all our contracts. But it was growing increasingly more evident to me that the only true peace for an individual is found at the center of God's perfect will for our lives. And it also became evident that the only way to achieve this peace is by being willing to surrender your entire life into the hands of your Creator.

I once heard a story about a guitarist who played a concert and received a standing ovation. The guitarist bowed and was greeted by his friend as he walked backstage.

"Go back out there! Everyone is clapping for you!" his friend said eagerly, slapping the guitarist on the back.

The guitarist peeked through the curtain, listening to the roar of a crowd whose applause was growing louder and louder with each second.

"See him?" the guitarist asked his friend, pointing at a man sitting in the front row, the only person in the auditorium who was not standing and clapping.

"Yeah," his friend said.

"He's not clapping, and he's my teacher."

If you please the world but don't please God, is it worth it?

This was my life for the longest time. For three decades, I was the guitarist listening to the roar of the crowd. And I feel that this addiction to pleasing people eventually contributed to warping my priorities.

Not once during my career had I looked at The Teacher sitting in the front row—waiting.

In my ignorance, I looked right past Him—for I hadn't thought about pleasing Him. I always thought He had other things to do— that my success while coming across as "a good person" must be pleasing to Him—and, really, I didn't feel like I needed Him until I went to heaven. All I cared about was winning games, making money, and listening to the crowd.

Looking back, this self-serving philosophy wore me out, re- sulted in a most exhausting and stressful lifestyle, and eventually led to my ruin. Praise and perceptions are enslaving only if your identity is wrapped up in them. Apparently, mine was. Champi- onships were never enough. Wins were never enough. Praise was never enough. Always, there was more of the world that I needed to conquer. So I needed to keep striving. I was busy writing my own story, and I always *had* to write something better. This striv- ing at its highest level eventually birthed an exhausting anxiety and aimless living. Eventually, it brought me down. Sometimes it takes brokenness to "grab our face mask" and get our attention, as my old football coach did when he wanted to make a point.

God revealed to me that for thirty years, I had essentially spent every waking hour of every day thinking only of what was best for me. I thought if I concentrated on my career and pushed myself to the hilt, then my effort would reward my family and benefit all those depending on me. But now, God was confronting me in or- der to teach me that, as Rick Warren admonished in *The Purpose Driven Life*, "It's not about me" any longer.

Modern coaches generally have a hard time thinking outside of themselves because their job can place them on a pedestal—and I was no different. I was learning now, however, that my new life needed to be all about Him and serving the Kingdom. I should be trying every day to honor God with all my thoughts, words, and actions—basically putting God, my Audience of One, at the very forefront of my being.

I don't think I ever would have slipped as I did if I had fully surrendered before and made Jesus Christ the Lord of my life. We will all inevitably still sin, but if we are truly abiding in God every day by continually surrendering, we will return again and again to the cross of Jesus Christ. Instead of returning again and again, I just kept drifting away.

Now, Full Surrender presented to me as an alternative offered me something entirely different. This newfound release began both hope and purpose starting to bloom in my soul, even without any signs of basketball on my horizon. This new paradigm was freeing me from my lifelong search for approval.

I was ready to embark on His greatest adventure for me. I decided it was never too late to start doing the right thing.

I was willing to believe that as a follower of Christ, my search for approval was over. My sole objective became getting right with God and my family. I found simply following Christ very fulfilling, even if I was a novice.

As I was getting started with Full Surrender and because of my lack of experience, I figured the only way I could implement this new concept was to start from scratch. It was as if God was making me into something new, that the Potter was starting all over again with me as the clay. I had "become like broken pottery" and "forgotten as though I were dead" (Psalm 31:12).

I once read that there must be Full Surrender before there can be Full Blessedness. When you take that leap of faith—and grant God your Full Surrender—one of two things will happen: God will either catch you, or He will teach you to fly. With me, He has done both.

With God behind your decisions, you feel a remarkable confidence, which, in turn, offers unspeakable joy—the inner peace that comes from obeying God. Proverbs 16:3 states: "Commit to the Lord whatever you do, and He will establish your plans."

In early 2007, I received a phone call from Gregg Lafitte, the husband of Claudia's college roommate, Jahn York. I had known Gregg because of this relationship, but also because Gregg's dad had been a great supporter of ours when I was at SMU. Gregg asked how I was, and we talked about our wives and then he asked if I would like to speak at the Salesmanship Club of Dallas, one of the largest service clubs in the nation. Formed in 1920, it consisted of over 600 Dallas business professionals; the club's desired focus was to make a positive impact on at-risk kids and families in north Texas. Not only would it be my first time speaking to a crowd in four years, but it would also be the first time I talked in front of people about my flaws and shortcomings.

I wasn't sure that my topic would be very interesting to the Club membership. Since Claudia didn't seem to object, I accepted. No matter my ignorance and arrogance before, my new goal was to focus on God. I was convinced God was behind this opportunity, that it was His way to get me back on track. If I truly believed in this idea of Full Surrender, I had no choice but to speak out.

And, since I'd be driving through Texas on my way from Denver to Dallas, I figured it was finally time that I give Bob Knight a call.

The last time I had seen Bob Knight was back in 2003, when his Texas Tech Red Raiders defeated our Baylor Bears in the Big 12 tournament, my final game as a head coach. Since then, communication had been scarce. He had invited me to his home in Lubbock, Texas, several times after the scandal, but I was too ashamed and still did not feel like I was ready. Finally, however, I wanted to reconnect.

I called him, and after a brief, upbeat conversation, it was decided: I would spend two days with Bob Knight in Lubbock on my way down to share my story in Dallas.

I experienced a wide range of emotions as I drove from Colorado down to Texas, but once I arrived in Lubbock, it felt as if Coach and I hadn't missed a beat. We recounted the same old stories with the same old punch lines that we had thirty years before. We also talked a great deal about basketball and his upcoming season with the Red Raiders. The next day, I sat in on his practice at Texas Tech; afterward, we analyzed his team and the strengths and weaknesses of each individual player. It felt like I was back in his office at Assembly Hall.

The following morning, we went to get some donuts at a local pastry shop in Lubbock. It was early and the regulars were just starting to congregate and get their coffee. When Coach walked in, all the customers noticed, and soon he was walking around the shop exchanging pleasantries. I couldn't help but feel as if I had gone back in time. It felt like I was back in Bloomington again—walking around Smitty's, one of his favorite luncheon stops.

It was nice to talk basketball and remember how it felt to laugh, but more than anything it was great to be back with Coach again. I smiled and thanked God for renewing our friendship. Our time together was far too brief, but it soon became time for me to pack my bags and see what God had in store for me in Dallas.

There were many things about the Salesmanship Club of Dallas speaking opportunity that made me hesitant and nervous. First of all, speaking so openly about my shortcomings was difficult enough when I was with Gary Lydic; doing it in a room filled with 600 people who already had negative perceptions of me was a whole new level of transparency.

As a coach, I was usually very comfortable speaking in public, but I knew this was going to be different. A month or so before my speech, I called my friend Zig Ziglar to run a few ideas by him.

He recommended I invite some of my closest friends so I could look over at them throughout my speech. He called it a "Table of Support."

He was right. The afternoon of my talk, I was heartened by the presence of the people at my "support" table. Gary Lydic flew in from Colorado Springs; and the rest of the table included SMU swimming coach George McMillion, Southwest Conference basketball referee Lynn Shortnacy, Eastfield College professor Bob Flickner, my neighbors from Waco, Royce Berger and Jim Bland, and Dallas sports talk host Norm Hitzges. Zig wasn't able to make it.

The afternoon talk was a surreal occasion. I thought back to all the times I had addressed many of the same people in the audience when I had been their alma mater's coach at Oklahoma, SMU, or Baylor. This was completely different, however, and whenever my emotions began to overcome me, I looked over at the table and immediately felt better. I'm not sure I remember all that I talked about that day because it was such a blur, but I shared from my heart what God was teaching me. I didn't hold back.

Although I wasn't sure what the people at the luncheon thought of my talk, I received a nice thank you note a couple weeks later from Gregg Lafitte. In the note, he mentioned: "Standing ovations are a rarity with our group. This was the first one in over a year." The only reason I share this is to show how much I felt God moved through the room that day and how much He strengthened me in my nervousness.

I was truly humbled by the entire experience, but as I look back I could see that the Salesmanship talk was not about me, but about how God was "nurturing" me. For the first time, I was beginning to believe that maybe God could turn my mess into some type of message.

But I also knew that it would only be possible if I was truly willing to continually surrender to Him.

GRACE

Lynn Shortnacy, who I mentioned being at my "Table of Support" at the Salesmanship Club of Dallas luncheon, was a referee friend of mine from back in my coaching days. I had known him for about twenty years, as he had "called" many games for Doug and me over the years at our various stops. In the fall of 2005, Lynn had reached out to me when I was at my depths.

I always thought Lynn was a good official, but I also recognized that he had a short fuse, so I usually left him alone during the game unless it was something extremely questionable. Over the years, we became pretty good friends because we had many similar friends and memories. I really enjoyed my relationship with most officials, especially after referee Bobby Dibler helped me institute an officiating school in conjunction with our Lobo Team Camp. The reason I enjoyed them was because I came to appreciate them as people, as well as respecting how difficult their job was.

Lynn became one of my best friends.

He was always encouraging and never wanted to hear me beat myself up. I appreciated that immensely because, although God was helping me feel better about myself, the reality of my past followed me wherever I went.

We spent countless hours talking about our newfound faith because he had experienced his own issues in his past as well. Together we formulated a new approach and decided to hold each other accountable so we wouldn't slip back into our old ways. We talked almost every day for five straight years, until Lynn died of brain cancer in April 2014.

Both of us found it fascinating how surrender simplified our lives. I had accepted that all of my striving had only cluttered my life and left me frustrated and confused. While writing in my journal one day, however, I started playing the devil's advocate and posed this question to myself: Was this new life paradigm just for someone who had seemingly ruined their life, or was surrender good for everyone?

I imagined people listening to my story and telling me, "Dave, you only surrendered because you had nowhere else to go." And I would certainly have to agree. I imagined other people saying, "Dave, you're like those guys who find God in prison." And I supposed this could be true, also. My follow-up to both of these queries, however, seemed to make sense to me.

If surrender was a good choice when all was falling down around me, why couldn't it also be a great choice when things were going well? Or, even better? The truism is that when things are going well, as they were for me, most people don't look for help because they feel they don't need it. That certainly was true in my case.

And then I got thinking: What makes this "surrender" so good for us, so perfect? The answer has to lie in the fact that the main ingredient in surrender is God's love. As I was learning almost daily about the magnitude His affection, it seemed only natural for one person to surrender to another whose only desire was to share His unconditional love. No agenda, just a desire for you to experience what is best for you. But I was hesitant all that time because I thought I knew what was better for me.

My sin and cover-up were not the only things I shared with King David. I, obviously, also shared his name. And the answer to why we should surrender, I believe, lies in the Hebrew meaning of the name David and I share.

Beloved.

The simple fact, however, is that we are *all* the beloved sons and daughters of God, no matter what we have done.

Yet, for my entire life, I had lived—I had *chosen* to live—in complete ignorance and avoidance of this relationship. It was that one-way thing again—I might have believed in God, I just didn't know how much He loved me. Until we realize the extent of this love, we can't trust it enough to surrender to Him.

What I was now learning enabled me to cautiously take the next step. After all I had been through, what did I have to lose? Would I rather keep relying on a foundation based on the inconsistencies of this world or switch to a reliance on a constant, loving Creator who always wants the best for you?

Also, if you believed that God's view of us was better than our own, which I now did, then doesn't it follow that His plan for us would be better than our own? All this caused me to believe that no matter what you think of yourself, God's view will always be better and it will be based solely on truth, not on performance or appearance. And this is why Full Surrender seems so beneficially valuable, even if your life has not catastrophically unraveled like mine.

My faith that an all-powerful, omniscient, sovereign, loving God was in charge of my future gave me a going-forward confidence—a confidence that, after everything at Baylor, I thought would be gone forever.

I was a long way from being over the hump and I was still hurting for my family. But I also knew that, although we weren't where we wanted to be, we were better than we had been.

My "fall from grace" had been a nightmare because of all the people I affected and everything I lost; but my "fall to grace" was proving equally difficult because I struggled to forgive myself for what I had done.

It was as if I was running along the shoreline of this thing called "grace," tempting the forgiving waves, but I was not able to fully dive into the crashing surf of complete forgiveness. Part of me was still trying to work my way back to acceptance, earn my forgiveness by my actions, and it was proving very frustrating and extremely futile. It's a tremendously radical idea—this mystery of grace!

Grace has been best defined as "the unmerited gift of God." I had heard previously that whereas mercy is God not doing to us what we do deserve, grace is God doing for us what we don't deserve—God's gift of forgiveness to a people who do not deserve it. After all I had put people through, all I had ruined, I certainly didn't feel I deserved unmerited forgiveness. And yet, God was calling me to view myself as He viewed me.

During my autopsy period, I read *Captured by Grace* by David Jeremiah, which follows the lives of John Newton, who wrote the hymn "Amazing Grace," and the Apostle Paul. John Newton was involved in the slave trade before he was touched by grace. The Apostle Paul persecuted and even murdered Christians before he was touched by grace. Even though these events happened centuries ago, I learned that grace still had, essentially, only two requirements: that we acknowledge we are totally contaminated, and that we are totally forgiven. I knew how totally I was contaminated; I struggled to believe I was forgiven.

Grace can change a life forever, as it did so profoundly for John Newton and the Apostle Paul. It was available to change me, too—but would I accept it? Would I accept God's opinion of me?

I kept reading, and, Old Testament or New, God's love was evident. I began to slowly become aware of God's pursuit of the human heart. It figuratively "peeled back my eyes," and a new level of consciousness began to form in my mind.

I saw why poet Francis Thompson wrote a poem about God titled "The Hound of Heaven." Ever since the fall in the Garden with Adam and Eve, God had been pursuing a people He cared for, restoring a relationship with the very people who disappointed Him time after time.

In fact, throughout the entire Old Testament, God is in pursuit. Not to say that there are never consequences for the Israelites' rebellion, but even His justice was an outpouring of His love because He cared enough to help His people get back on track. Therefore, if His pursuit is love and His justice is love, I theorized that love must be at the very core of who God is.

By now I was realizing that this is what God was doing with me the whole time—He was chasing me. And although He had to chasten me for my bad decisions, He was teaching me that even though He was very big, He was small enough to care about my life. This was a major change in my view of God—He, who was powerful enough to create the universe, had the desire to walk with me daily.

I had read "The Parable of the Lost Son" in Luke 15:11-32 numerous times—"The Prodigal Son," as it is commonly called. During my period of trying to understand God's gift of grace, the story had a profound impact on me. In the parable, the lost son takes his father's inheritance and squanders it on wild living. Losing it all, the lost son hits rock bottom, so much so that he finds himself in squalor, eating with pigs. He realizes that even his father's servants are better off than he is, so he decides to return home.

As I read, I could identify with each shameful step of his journey back home. His life in ruins, I imagined him practicing his apology over and over in his head as he shuffled up the path to his father's house. He probably expected his father to be so angry and ashamed of him that he would probably disown him—which would certainly be deserved.

But as the lost son approaches his father's property, the father sees him from a distance and runs to meet his son. Luke 15:21-24 says:

> *The son said to him, "Father, I have sinned against heaven and against you. I am no longer worthy to be called your son."*

But the father said to his servants, "Quick! Bring the best robe and put it on him. Put a ring on his finger and sandals on his feet. Bring the fattened calf and kill it. Let's have a feast and celebrate. For this son of mine was dead and is alive again; he was lost and is found." So they began to celebrate.

I understood that Jesus told the story as a metaphor for how God views us. God the Father runs after us to meet his lost sons. And I wondered: Is this what God was doing with me?

The same man who told that parable also said, "Oh, ye of little faith." He was talking to me there, too. Whereas we as humans have difficulty forgiving if we are hurt by another person, God's reaction is completely the opposite. He opens up His arms to meet us, and not only that, He meets us exactly where we are at the time we are broken. Though we may all be on a line from A to Z in our various lives, God meets us perfectly; if we're at E, He'll meet us at E; if we're at O, He'll meet us at O; if we're at Z, He'll meet us at Z. He loves us so much that He will meet us right where we are in that moment, but He also loves us too much to leave us there. He wants to show us that there is a better place, a home, for us.

The more I read, the more I understood that the entire Bible was a narrative of God, time after time, restoring His relationship with His people. God was the one restoring, however, not the people. And the people weren't changing for God; they were changing *because* of Him. It was His love and grace that called them to follow.

Was this the grace I had always heard about? Was I experiencing the undeserved love of God at a time in my life when I felt like I least deserved it?

Gradually, I realized that what mattered most was not what others might say about my life, but what God said about it and how my family felt. The world was telling me, "Bliss, you're worthless;" and I was telling myself, "Dave, you're worthless;" but God was saying, "David, you are my beloved, and I have more for you to do."

I've mentioned there were four things David expressed in Psalm 51.
- **First, his admission of guilt.** I had done that; I felt horrible about what I had done.
- **Second, his complete break from sin.** I had done that; I was determined to get back on track and try to earn trust back from everyone I loved.
- **Third, his broken spirit.** I certainly had experienced all that; all I had to offer now was my broken self and shattered life.
- But the fourth requirement—**the accepting of God's forgiveness and reinstatement**—was where I was at and became my biggest struggle in my recovery. I struggled to shake off my guilt.

Then one morning I read C.S. Lewis. Essentially, he said that if God forgives us, we must forgive ourselves; to not forgive ourselves would indicate that we feel we are more important than God.

As I struggled with the acceptance of God's grace, I read Max Lucado's, *Facing Your Giants*, and realized that the giant in my own life was my guilt.

Although I was now willing to believe that God loved me, it still didn't remove the fact that I hated what I had done. Guilt, at its core, is the inability to forgive oneself. The evil one wanted to use my guilt as his primary tool to prevent me from ever making something worthwhile of my life again. Guilt appeared to stand in opposition to grace. Guilt's stated goal is to blind you from grace.

I was learning, however, that guilt is not the same as conviction. Conviction is healthy, and it leads to repentance. It's an introspective look and examination of one's life, and having a good understanding of your weaknesses is one of the first steps in sanctification. Guilt, however, is the continual internal self-deprecation over something you have done, something in your past, something that God has already forgiven you for. It was this guilt that was constantly trying to discourage me.

Max Lucado went on to say that the devil deals in two commodities: guilt of the past and temptation of the future. Both of these shift your eyes from the Audience of One and put them back on yourself and your shortcomings. When all you see are your shortcomings, how can you see the gospel?

It is the devil's intention to win twice, both going and coming. He wants to distract you from your purpose and watch you fall (Victory #1), and then he wants your guilt to keep you from ever coming back to purpose again (Victory #2). He likes it when we carry this guilt because this keeps us away from God's grace. The devil knows God can make something good from a bad situation, which would then be a testament to His goodness. The sad truth is that the enemy wants to steal our joy.

But this is where God's grace triumphantly comes to the rescue of all sinners.

Whereas guilt wants to burden you, grace wants to propel you back into His purposes for your life. There were times I was drowning in guilt and all I wanted to do was disappear because of all the sorrow I caused the very people I loved the most.

This was the relentless battle throughout my restoration—a tug-of-war of sorts between grace and guilt. Oftentimes it felt like I'd take two steps forward in my recovery, but my guilt would make me take one step back. Frankly, guilt will always be a struggle, but in order to avoid succumbing to arrogance again, I had to accept Jesus' death as a sacrifice for my sinful actions.

Earlier, I posed the question: How can you forgive yourself when you're reminded of your depravity each and every day? Somehow, that answer lies in grace, believing there *is* something bigger than you that dwarfs your depravity. I was learning that grace was demonstrated most in the cross of Jesus Christ, towering high above my sin. I had been looking back at my depravity instead of looking up and realizing what the cross was all about. When I finally understood this, I saw my sin cower in the enormous shadow of the cross. The cross is the greatest demonstration of grace this world has ever known. All of a sudden the humiliation of my sin was replaced by the joy that flowed from a relationship available in Jesus Christ.

Jesus' death on the cross reminds us that God isn't surprised at our sin, but in fact has made provision for them. When we sin and ask forgiveness and then repent, God forgives us and only sees the purity of His Son. Like the story of "The Prodigal Son," the Father is the one running to meet us through the death of His Son—His arms wide open.

Grace does not say, "Change before you enter the throne room." Grace says, "Come to the throne room just as you are and allow this scandalous love to change you from within."

Henri Nouwen, in his book *Life of the Beloved*, says: "Self-rejection is the greatest enemy of the spiritual life because it contradicts the sacred voice that calls us the 'Beloved.' Being the Beloved expresses the core truth of our existence."

And, though it was a battle, I was beginning to awaken to this magnificent and mysterious concept of grace. The more I read my Bible, the more I began to accept that maybe God's perception of me was better than my own. The self-hatred I had harbored for so long was finally beginning to be replaced with glorious God-discovery.

The God of grace I was now reading about in the Bible, I found, was far different than the God I believed in for the first sixty years of my life—the Straitjacket Santa Claus who was a distant, restrictive disciplinarian.

Before, I had difficulty believing that God cared 24/7 about my life and that He actually wanted to take the time to help direct events in my life. Now, as I read the Bible, I saw how wrong I was.

How could I have been that ignorant of my importance to God, my significance to God, when Matthew 10:30 says that "the very hairs of your head are all numbered"? I hadn't taken the time to discover who God was and how much He wanted to be part of my life.

I had approached my faith more as a business proposition than a relationship. This sounds horrible, but I almost feel that I viewed my salvation like a "Get Into Heaven Free" card. God was nice to have on your side; He was good insurance, you know, to make sure I got into heaven, but He was not someone who really had time to care about me 24/7. But now, standing in the wonder of grace, my view of God was expanding.

My entire life, I had missed out on this. I think there are a couple of reasons why. First of all, because of my understanding of the human concept of time and dimension, man can't be in two places at once; therefore, without reading my Bible, I had no understanding of God's omnipresence. I was now aware that God is not restricted by time or space. And second, man sometimes thinks he can orchestrate his own life pretty well, without the help of God; I believed this, too. I had a beautiful wife, three healthy children, and I was a college basketball coach with a pretty good record. Why would I need God? Ignorance in the first example and arrogance in the second set me up for an eventual fall.

But there is no doubt that my brokenness before God and full surrender to Him forced me to look at things differently. I had ample time to meditate on this new theory, and it started to make wonderful sense. Not only did it make sense, but I also began to start seeing God's hand working in my life, even in the depths of my depression. Day by day, the personal, Christian God of grace was changing my thinking. I couldn't help feeling that maybe He was changing me, too.

My significance was beginning to take on a new identity. It was beginning to come from my relationship with God and not what I had done in this world. And I was beginning to rest in the consistent and unchanging nature of a God who called me His beloved.

22
DAWN

As mentioned earlier, in the summer of 2003, I was a coach on a Big 12 All-Star basketball trip to Scandinavia. At one point during the trip, we took a cruise ship from Oslo, Norway to Copenhagen, Denmark. When we arrived in Copenhagen, the massive ship, in an attempt to park in the harbor, had to turn completely around and back into its slip, so as to be headed out in anticipation of the next day's trip. The entire process went very slowly and, although the movement was almost indiscernible, at the end of a two-hour period, the ship was facing the outward direction, ready for a return voyage.

That's how my recovery was for me. Making a similar 180-degree change in my thinking was also a time-consuming and sometimes an almost indiscernible process.

After speaking to the Salesmanship Club of Dallas in the fall of 2007, I was invited shortly thereafter by Athletes in Action (AIA) to speak to coaches at the Final Four in San Antonio, Texas. After a four-year hiatus that oftentimes felt hopeless, I couldn't believe what the Lord was beginning to do with my life.

San Antonio was always one of my favorite spots for the Final Four because of the city's great hospitality. Most NCAA coaches convene at the Final Four for meetings and events, even if their team is not participating.

My talk was on the Friday afternoon preceding the first games and took place in a large auditorium in an interview format with TNT's Ernie Johnson. The two of us sat on an elevated stage, which allowed me to look out on the standing-room-only sea of approximately 500 people. Most were coaches. Some were former players. All of them were curious.

My memory of the occasion was that Ernie was his usual great self and that, somehow, I got through it without breaking down too much.

I led off by saying something that I really believed.

"None of you would do something as foolish as what I did," I told them. "But you have to understand: I didn't think I would, either."

It was both humbling and a bit humiliating perhaps to stand in front of those who were members of the very profession I had shamed. But if this was what the Lord had in store for me, I was willing to obey. It was not about rebuilding my reputation anymore; it was about taking care of my family and being available to help and encourage others. Whatever His purpose was for me, I was determined to do it, despite perceptions and despite the newspaper articles that came with showing my face in public again.

Showing my face in basketball circles did bring in a new wave of media attention. Many articles bashed Athletes in Action for allowing me an opportunity to speak about ethics and questioned whether I had actually changed. To my own surprise, the negative publicity didn't anger me as it once would have because I was no longer trying to get my coaching job back. This time I wanted to sincerely encourage people to guard their priorities.

The talk lasted about an hour and seemed well received, but I felt a great deal of anguish being back in my old basketball setting. As I watched the Final Four games the next day, I couldn't help but reflect back a few short years before when I was part of the wonderful spectacle. But then I remembered: *I am on a different career path now.* I snapped out of it.

And, although my life appeared to be taking on a different purpose, there still were issues on the home front with my family that I wanted to resolve.

As terrible as I felt during the period immediately after we moved to Colorado, it had to be worse for Claudia. She experienced the depression and humiliation that accompanied the Baylor scandal, but moving her back to her home area of Denver, thinking that it would be a safe haven, only served to further embarrass her.

Overall, it was difficult to lose a life we had lived for so long. Basketball wasn't *my* thing; it was *our* thing. Over the years, for example, one of her favorite things to do was have the players over for dinner. In many ways, as with most coaches, our players felt like our children. She was great as a coach's wife, and we loved the coaching life. We always assumed coaching would go on forever.

So, when it all came tumbling down, the pain was enormous. For both of us.

For the next couple of years after Jeff left for college, Claudia and I were continually challenged, as Christians, to stay the course. We both came from fundamentalist families where divorce was not an option, but it was difficult to imagine a time when we would ever be able to smile again. Fueled by the strength of others, including our kids, we tried to just hang in there and hope the storm would one day pass. And, there was a heartening new form of faith for me. Just as I now knew God was the only way I could be restored, I also believed that the same God could also resurrect our struggling marriage.

During this period, God selected another man to help save our relationship—my brother-in-law, Randy Miller. Along with Gary Lydic, he was a true friend who pointed Claudia and me toward truth.

Randy, who worked in commercial real estate, was an encourager to everyone with whom he interacted. He had grown deep in his faith and, although he wasn't a pastor, he had a great sensitivity in faith issues. He would participate in marriages, baptisms, dedications, etc. A real gift of his was coming alongside people who were in distress, comforting them with his caring heart, and counseling them with his scriptural knowledge.

He was great for me. The first thing he told me was to be truthful with God if I expected Him to help me. In addition, Randy introduced me to the concept of the devil and spiritual warfare.

I had always viewed the devil as some sort of comical character and even remember that Bob Knight had a devil on the cover of his defensive pamphlet from the late 1960s. The menacing cartoon figure on Coach's notebook was in a defensive stance and really getting after it. Randy explained to me that very little had changed, that the devil had done a number on me, and now he was really getting after our marriage.

Randy led me through references in the Bible about the devil and how he would take our human insecurities and sinful nature and trick us into actions that dishonored our respect for God. In a nutshell, I became very conscious of my daily actions.

Randy would also pray over Claudia and me; I really feel this helped us immeasurably. He also recommended a terrific book about marriage, *Discovering The Mind of a Woman* by Ken Nair. I listened to everything Randy said and was committed to not giving up.

Just as I experienced during my autopsy with God, I also learned about the areas that had gone wrong in our marriage in the four or five years that followed scandal. Much of this revolved around my inability to move on.

I hadn't held a real steady job since the days at Gart's Sporting Goods, five years prior. I initially took that job primarily to get out of the house, but I did well enough to be offered a managerial position after six months. My frustration with the low pay, however, caused me to pursue several other questionable ventures that promised to help us "hit it big" financially. I say questionable because they certainly weren't what you might expect from an Ivy League graduate. After sustaining an affluent lifestyle for the past twenty years, I was now groping for something that would return us to that previous status. But all these forays into start-up companies and MLMs merely served to disillusion me and frustrate Claudia even more.

She originally had wanted me to take the Gart's position, but I felt I was too old to pursue that route. If I had been ten to fifteen years younger, it would have been more feasible, but now I was in a big hurry to get back to making a six-figure income. As I went from idea to idea, I would feel she was being negative toward my attempts to get our lives back on track. In reality, though, she was just disappointed that I wasn't doing something better with my time. Certainly my wrongdoing at Baylor had caused her tremendous embarrassment and humiliation, but my repeated attempts to find a "get-rich-quick" job only furthered these feelings.

There is little doubt that if I had just lost my job at Baylor merely because I couldn't win enough games, I probably would have been able to re-cycle in basketball at some level and still be in coaching. However, because my exit featured a complete lack of integrity, as well as the disturbing tapes, I was a persona non grata. No one, with the exception of the CBA's Dakota Wizards, would touch me.

Therefore, a lot of jobs for which I may have been qualified, I never even applied for because I was too ashamed and embarrassed. This prevented me from some of the auxiliary positions normally available to out-of-work coaches—such as sales, public relations, or announcing. No one was interested in the "pariah."

Consequently, with nothing legitimate available on the job front, I gravitated to the "get-rich-quick" schemes. I have to give it to those people, though, because they do a good job of luring you in with their promises of high income and a luxurious lifestyle. One of my lowest moments occurred when I was pedaling one of these programs at the Texas Association of Basketball Coaches (TABC) clinic in San Antonio. Back in my coaching days, the TABC had presented me with a couple of Texas College Coach of the Year plaques. Now I was hawking a mortgage reduction program out of a sales booth at their convention. Don't get me wrong—there was nothing wrong with the program, but there was a lot wrong with my attitude.

With me just bouncing from one scheme to another, it was difficult for Claudia to see how I was moving forward. And if I wasn't moving forward, what hope did she have for our future? This put tremendous stress on our marriage because, although I might want to get into something respectable, I hadn't come to grips with forgiving myself at the time, so I was reluctant to try. I still was operating under the weight of tremendous guilt and it kept me from pursuing a legitimate job.

Therefore, what I perceived as her lack of forgiveness was mostly a result of understandable disappointment in my inability to move forward. My inability to move forward was a result of the guilt I harbored over the wrongdoings in Waco. She was upset that I didn't have a better plan, but I didn't have a better plan because I didn't think I deserved a better plan.

Consequently, I wallowed in the quicksand of mediocrity and self-pity for several years. As I look back, I am extremely disappointed that I wasn't stronger for my family than I was. I was spinning my wheels, looking for a quick fix so that I could take care of my family financially, but I hadn't helped them at all emotionally. It wasn't until I started reading about the grace of God that I made any headway at all.

Before an airplane takes off, flight attendants normally ask passengers to fasten their seatbelts and make sure seats and table trays are in an upright position. Then, they usually give instructions on how to use your oxygen mask in case of loss of cabin pressure. They instruct passengers to put the mask on themselves first before helping anyone else. This was always interesting to me. Obviously, the point was that if you didn't secure your mask, you might not be able to help others. Once you were secure, however, it would be safe to help others.

This was exactly what God was now telling me: "Put the oxygen mask on, accept My grace." There I was, struggling in the quagmire of guilt, and He was offering His grace and forgiveness, if I would just put the mask on. After years of struggling with this concept, I finally understood what He was offering. As soon as I put on the mask of "His Grace," everything changed for me.

The more I depended on God, the more I saw the work of His hand in my life.

Looking back over the first sixty years of my life, I enjoyed an overflow of professional and personal blessings. But when the Baylor situation occurred, I receded into a shell because of my shame and remorse. But now, when all was in shambles, I felt His love like never before, for I had been awakened.

Over the next few years, I believe God gave Claudia and me a number of wonderful occurrences to help mend our hurt. Robert got married to Laura, an amazing daughter-in-law, and I thanked the Lord. Berkeley got married to James, an amazing son-in-law, and I thanked the Lord. Jeff graduated from NYU Film School and went to California to seek his dream, and I thanked the Lord. Four grandchildren came into the world, and this brought Claudia and me great joy.

It was as if God was cocooning our marriage in His love by surrounding us with the people that mattered the most to us. Life seemed to gradually become less and less about what I had lost, and more about how God was going to provide. His mercies were new every morning (Lamentations 3:23). Just as a plant is dependent on a drenching rain from above, I was becoming more and more dependent on God's "drenching" love.

My life had finally slowed down, and I could fully appreciate the family God had blessed me with. I've heard it said that if you are too busy to hunt or fish, you are too busy, and for sixty years, I had been too busy to do a lot of things that would have been good for me.

What surprised me about this period was that despite my circumstances, I began to be aware of the daily blessings that I used to take for granted. Now I found myself attempting to be in constant union with God, thanking Him for His loving guidance in our lives. I began asking God about everything, no matter how insignificant, because I wanted Him to know that I valued this newfound input.

I found that true peace came from not compromising. My Audience of One was fulfilling His end of the bargain, and I began to understand what Ephesians 6:18 meant by "pray in the Spirit on all occasions." Prayer was no longer something I did to check off my list or put forth my "Christian" front. Prayer became more important than ever, and I saw my prayers being answered.

Although Claudia and I are still working our way back, even to this day, I know that with God's help, we can get there. We have survived the hard part and have stayed together. I know we would not have made it if it weren't for God's grace. Life's circumstances tried to rip us a part—this is what the devil wanted—but God's grace empowered us to work our way back.

Finally, nearly a half-decade after the scandal, Claudia and I decided to leave Denver and return to the place that always felt like home for us: Texas, U.S.A.

It's said that it is always darkest before the dawn.

HOPE

The 1994 film *The Shawshank Redemption* is a story of hope and purpose. Film critic Roger Ebert, now deceased, said the film is "an allegory about holding onto a sense of personal worth, despite everything." The film's story is told in the context of the relationship between Andy Dufresne (Tim Robbins) and "Red" Redding (Morgan Freeman), two inmates at Shawshank Prison.

Andy is hopeful in his nature; Red cautions Andy against it. "Let me tell you something, my friend," Red says to Andy while they are in prison. "Hope is a dangerous thing. Hope can drive a man insane."

Andy, who has been falsely convicted of murdering his wife and sentenced to life at Shawshank, miraculously breaks out of prison. Before his breakout, however, Andy tells Red about a location in Maine where he asked his wife to marry him. He then tells Red about hiding something in a long rock wall near that location.

Once Red serves the remainder of his sentence, he is released from prison and journeys to find the rock wall Andy spoke of. In the wall is a box, and inside is a letter from Andy. In the letter is a line that reads: "Remember, Red, hope is a good thing, maybe the best of things, and no good thing ever dies."

If the Old Testament was truly a chronicling God's pursuit of a people He loves (Israel), and if the New Testament was the climax of that pursuit through the life, ministry, and crucifixion of Jesus Christ, then it would make sense for such a great demonstration of His love to be stamped with some great occurrence that backs up all the divine claims Jesus made.

That great occurrence is one of the most hopeful things of mankind: Jesus did not remain in the tomb.

Three days after His crucifixion, He conquered death and left an empty tomb behind Him. If Jesus had not risen from the dead, we would never know if He was a deranged lunatic or truly was the Son of God. Even His resurrection was an outpouring of God's love because it proved to us the reality of the Messiah. And if Christ could defeat sin on the cross and conquer death through His resurrection, I realized it should give me hope that He could help me move past my own sin and help me resurrect my own life, as well.

A new understanding of this resurrection gave me hope for the future.

If conquering death isn't enough, I learned that the Christian message gets even more hopeful. Just as my brother-in-law, Randy Miller, helped rescue me from my ignorance of the devil, he did the same thing in educating me about the Holy Spirit.

"The Holy Spirit is not a bronze medal winner," I remember Randy telling me. "He is part of the God-head—every bit as important as God and Jesus."

I learned that Jesus came to establish our union with the Father, and when He ascended into heaven, He left His followers with Something equally fulfilling—Someone who would live in us and through us, available every hour of every day.

If nothing else, this removed any thoughts I had about my "distant" God metaphor. How can the Holy Spirit, with its 24/7 availability, be an afterthought? Was this the same "Holy Ghost" I had recited in memorized prayers when I was younger? In John 14, though the disciples probably did not understand at the time, Jesus promises the coming of "another advocate" to be with them forever—"the Spirit of truth."

Jesus was saying that after He was no longer on this earth, the Holy Spirit, the Third Person of the Trinity, would come as a Comforter, Teacher, and Helper to be with those who are wholeheartedly following Him. In Matthew 28:20, before He ascends into heaven after His resurrection, Jesus says this: "And surely I am with you always, to the very end of the age." I learned that this is fulfilled through the Spirit.

I found tremendous hope in this. We are in Christ, and He is in us. The Creator of the universe loves us so much that He has unleashed His Spirit to do a work in us and, equally important, through us. It's as if, in the arms of brokenness and surrender, the Spirit partners with our God-given passions and works through us to make something beautiful from our shattered lives.

It was as if Randy had helped me discover an entirely new being, this Spirit of Truth. And it gave me even more hope.

I have learned that inner fruit is God's call upon us to allow the Spirit to work within and transform us into the image of His Son while outer fruit is God's call upon us to declare His truth and meet the needs of those who come across our path. The Spirit had to do a work in me (inner fruit) before He did something through me (outer fruit). As I came before God's throne in surrender, day in and day out, some days better than others, I noticed that my natural abilities resurfaced.

I thought more about God in my five-year post-scandal period than I had in my previous sixty years combined. One time, I was listening to Paul Young, author of *New York Times* bestseller *The Shack*, and he said, "What you focus on expands." This was certainly true in my spiritual life—the more I focused on God, the more my understanding of Him expanded. This allowed me to feel more confident about His purpose for me than ever before, though I still had a long way to go.

Rick Warren says in *The Purpose Driven Life* that when you grow closer to God, He will give you a passion for something He cares deeply about so you can be a spokesman for Him to the world. I didn't know about being any spokesman, but I could feel life being breathed back into me.

The Potter had His way with me for five long years before I started to feel meaning again. It became apparent that God was interested in the process of changing what I desired far more than He was interested in the process of giving me what I desired. He could do either, and giving would be simpler, but changing was obviously better.

As I continued to grow in the understanding of grace, I felt a tremendous responsibility to continually examine my motives. I could see that it would be far too easy to end up right back where I started, and that was a terrifying thought. I had to realize that everything I did from now on—each opportunity I was given to impact someone—had to be for God's glory. I could not return to my previous lifestyle of people-pleasing and constructing my own Tower of Babel. There was no other way to achieve His will without committing to Full Surrender, with the realization that my life was no longer my own to live.

When I spoke to people, I did not want to be just another cliché redemption story everyone has already heard. I did not want to come off as being another sports figure who found God. I also didn't want anything to do with the self-promotion of the "new me" or for anyone to think that I was only using God again as a means to accomplish my purposes.

By allowing God to produce my inner fruit, I was hoping it would reflect outwardly how repentant I was.

I believe that there may be no greater feeling than the existence of hope. Everyone needs it at some time or another; sick people need it, poor people need it, and wounded spirits need it. Without hope, all is emptiness.

During my coaching days, I became very cognizant of the importance of never leaving a losing locker-room without creating the expectation of renewed hope for tomorrow. I always felt that the team needed it, and so did the coaches.

I once went to a conference where successful businesswoman and speaker Edie Varley told the audience, "The most valuable renewable resource in the world is the human spirit." I agree with her completely. The only thing I would add is the element of hope to the human spirit.

I have discovered that with hope, the spirit flourishes. Hope starts at the foot of the cross by humbly surrendering pride and self and accepting love and grace. I adopted 1 Timothy 1:12-16 as my rallying cry:

> *I thank Christ Jesus our Lord, who has given me strength, that he considered me trustworthy, appointing me to his service. Even though I was once a blasphemer and a persecutor and a violent man, I was shown mercy because I acted in ignorance and unbelief. The grace of our Lord was poured out on me abundantly, along with the faith and love that are in Christ Jesus. Here is a trustworthy saying that deserves full acceptance: Christ Jesus came into the world to save sinners—of whom I am the worst. But for that very reason I was shown mercy so that in me, the worst of sinners, Christ Jesus might display his immense patience as an example for those who would believe in him and receive eternal life.*

The understanding of Easter Sunday and the outpouring of the Holy Spirit continued to work on my heart. I remember thinking that the Apostle Peter probably thought his denial and betrayal of Jesus was how his relationship with Christ was going to end—especially the moment Christ was crucified. How depressed would Peter have been for the rest of his life if that were how his relationship with Jesus ended? But then Jesus rose from the dead and before He ascended into heaven, Jesus propelled Peter into purpose, saying to him, "Feed my sheep."

Similar to Peter, I hoped I could be useful again. The resurrection and indwelling of the Holy Spirit gave me a "living hope" because it implied there was a loving God that could conquer all that contained me, such as sin and guilt. Because we are so imperfect and this world is so imperfect, circumstances can cause people to lose hope, as I had. But God never looks at a situation as if it's hopeless. That's when God does his best work. He is still a God of miracles who relishes the opportunity to restore lives—I hoped He would continue to restore mine.

As I began to go public with my story—essentially a story of God's strength in my weaknesses—it was the resurrection and Holy Spirit that fueled my hope, and hope that was renewing my spirit.

I think Andy Dufresne in *The Shawshank Redemption* was right!

"Hope was a good thing, maybe the best of things, and no good thing ever dies."

COME BACK

Though my renewed hope was helping me turn the corner, I wondered what was next.

Upon our move back to Texas, I remember being hit with a wave of sadness on June 22, the first day in the summer solstice. For the last several years, I'd been feeling anxiety around this time. June 21 was the longest day of the year, and that meant the sun was starting its journey back south until it reached its southern most limits on December 21. Over the coming months, the days would be getting shorter as the Texas sun slept a little bit more each day.

I'm not sure why this sadness always fell upon me this time of the year, but perhaps it was a reminder that just about everything in life is temporary. My sinful acts, I figured, had swallowed up a significant percent of my life that I could have been coaching, and I guess I felt like I was running out of time. Although I was enjoying my opportunities to share my story, I wasn't getting any younger, and I couldn't help but wonder how much time I had remaining. What was next for me?

My new understanding of grace, however, buoyed me during these moments of doubt and gave me confidence not to worry. I now fully believed that a God who loved me was now in control and would direct my steps if I allowed Him to do so.

Although my life might have changed dramatically, I was learning that my purpose was still alive.

The word "comeback" means to return to a place of significance or a place that was lost for a period of time.

Every year, in many of the professional sports leagues, there is a "Comeback Player of the Year" award given out. It is usually presented to an athlete who has distinguished himself for a period of years, but then suffers a setback that causes him to have an off season. His performance suffers and his statistics reflect a very sub-par performance. Then in the following year he bounces back to regain his high level of play. For this resurgence, he is presented with "Comeback Player of the Year" honors. This award is voted on by the media and, although there may be several candidates, there is only one winner.

It seemed that in the Christian life, a "Comeback" award would also be very special, and although many people pass judgment on the candidates, only one person does the voting: God. And He gives this award out every day to those who will approach His throne on their knees with a repentant spirit and an attitude of surrender.

In my own life, I was learning that this was not a "comeback" (noun) as the world might see it; rather, it was a "come back" (verb) to God so that He could orchestrate His plans in my life. My disappointment in my actions and behavior was genuine, and I was now determined to cooperate with God and allow Him to change me from the inside-out. If what I read in Romans was true, and I believed it was—that all have sinned and come short of the glory of God—then I and everyone else must all constantly come back from whatever sin it is that hinders our relationship with Him. I've heard it said that the Christian life is a series of new beginnings, and I, too, hoped God would give me a new beginning. I had to come back to God so He could orchestrate a pure, Christ-centered comeback for me.

In *The Purpose Of Man*, author A.W. Tozer talks about how the real tragedy in the Garden of Eden was not Satan's convincing Adam and Eve to sin, but how Adam and Eve lost their purpose of bringing joy and pleasure to God and enjoying Him for themselves. I had learned that Satan will defiantly offer anything to keep us from glorifying God. He will offer substitutes and compromises that seem very attractive but are very shortsighted. He did this in the Garden, and he did this with me.

I learned that when we forget our true purpose of glorifying God in our thoughts, words, and deeds, it is a kind of "spiritual amnesia." In my life, it was a complete misunderstanding about the existence of God's love that caused me to lose the real vision of God's purpose in my life. I thought I knew my purpose, but I was just spinning my wheels, selfishly pursuing the success that the world was selling.

However, continual communion with God allows us to maintain open communication with Him as He reveals His purposes for us, thus allowing us to break our sin patterns before they lead to a disastrous fall. It makes us sensitive to His every stimulus because we are walking in the Holy Spirit. In sports terms, walking in the Spirit produces protection (our defense) and power (our offense), combining for a purpose-filled life (our victory).

Perhaps the most quoted passage in regard to God having a plan and purpose for our lives is Jeremiah 29:11:

> *"For I know the plans I have for you," declares the Lord, "plans to prosper you and not to harm you, plans to give you hope and a future."*

That verse really gave me hope in the early days of my depression in 2003, but, as time went on, I found that the next three verses in Jeremiah were just as important:

> *"Then you will call on me and come and pray to me, and I will listen to you. You will seek me and find me when you seek me with all your heart. I will be found by you," declares the Lord, "and will bring you back from captivity. I will gather you from all the nations and places where I have banished you," declares the Lord, "and will bring you back to the place from which I carried you into exile."*

I couldn't help but notice all the verbs in Jeremiah 29:12-14: call, come, pray, seek, find, and seek (again). As we act, God also acts. Perhaps He wanted to give me the right things, but, more than that, He wanted me to *want* the right things. As a result of seeking Him, God says, "I will be found by you."

This fellowship with Him helped me know Him better. I actually felt like I *needed* Jesus—each and every day. I prayed earnestly for God to take over my life. Slowly, but surely, I could feel my spirit changing for the better. Was this what the Bible meant by "abiding"? Maybe "abiding" and "comeback" went hand-in-hand.

An interesting thought came to me one morning on my routine walk around my neighborhood. I had just finished reading *The Blessings of Brokenness* by Charles Stanley, and Stanley said there could be tremendous results provided the person who was broken had the proper response. It seemed, therefore, if I was willing to accept this brokenness as a necessary part of God's course-correction in my life, then it seemed incumbent upon me to at least attempt to come back, as good-faith recognition of His loving chastisement. My comeback attempt, however, would not be for *my* purpose; it would be for the benefit of what God could then do through my salvaged life.

God had already reconstructed so much of my being, including giving me a brand new identity and revitalized purpose. He had admonished me through my autopsy; He had awakened me to the extent of His love; and now He had introduced me to His grace by helping me understand the benefits of brokenness.

These preliminary steps were all setting the stage for my comeback, but the last step was up to me, as it always seems to be with God. Because I had never committed to anything like this before, I knew the final step would require a complete leap of faith. But as I reflected back on all the positive things that were starting to occur in my life, it seemed that I owed it to Him to at least try this comeback. Maybe it would show God that I was repentant for my actions and appreciative of His grace now abounding in my life.

I also felt that if I didn't even attempt to come back or, even worse, tried to go back to doing things on my own again, it would be a slap in God's face, communicating to Him that I didn't really believe in Him.

By now, however, I realized that this comeback would have nothing to do with my returning to my old life, but everything to do with returning to God's plan for my life. It convinced me that the central component of any comeback for a Christian must have a spiritual dimension to it. It must be redemptive.

The truth is, as much as I yearned for a comeback during the first couple of years after my indiscretion, that comeback would have been based on selfish thinking and getting back to where I had been before: winning games, making money, and going to the NCAA post-season tournament. In other words, that type of comeback would have been all about me and what I could re-attain.

God's idea about my comeback was completely different and wouldn't be a testament to me at all. This was, in fact, a testament to a God of forgiveness, grace, and redemption who wouldn't give up on me.

That is why I have felt that He took my piece off the playing board of life—I simply wasn't ready for a comeback. Just as the potter in Jeremiah 18 reworks the clay vessel, God had to "rework" me and prepare me for my second chance.

Rick Warren's *The Purpose Driven Life* helped me fully understand this point. He says that our second chance will most likely be completely different from what we might anticipate, but it also might be infinitely better than anything we can imagine—that is, if we obey God every step of the way. Warren also says that our comeback probably would not be in the timetable we would prefer because there are a lot of changes that have to take place in the various areas of our lives—like our attitudes, thinking, friends, and habits. I have experienced this exact phenomenon as God continually refined me in the years following the scandal.

And, although there might be changes in my life, thankfully one thing did not change—and that was God. He was, as Hebrews 13:8 says, "the same yesterday and today and forever." As I contemplated this principle, I derived a great deal of confidence from it. If I believed all that was in the Bible, as I now was committed to believing, then perhaps God would do with me what He had done in so many characters in the stories I had read, like King David.

I was encouraged to believe that coming back to God's purpose in my life might still be possible.

Apparently God wasn't finished completely with my "coming out" because a week after my talk to the coaches at the Final Four in San Antonio, Mo Michalski ("Coach Mo") from Athletes In Action called me and asked if I would like to coach AIA's USA team in the Jones Cup in Taipei, Taiwan. In addition to coaching again, I would get to take Claudia along with me on the trip.

In the past, prior to 2008, because it is not a "high-profile" world competition, the USA Basketball Committee allowed a minor league professional group (perhaps from the CBA) to represent America in the Jones Cup. However, that didn't work out, and AIA was given the opportunity to organize a team that would represent America in a better light. This is how AIA became involved and continues to be involved in this way today.

We invited twelve players to train for six days, and my entire team was made up of faith-based players. It was amazing to watch as the selected ten players all "rowed in the same direction." We had some pretty good players: Da'Sean Butler and Wellington Smith from West Virginia, and Brett Winkelman and Ben Woodside from North Dakota State. It was a great experience. We lost to Jordan in the first game, and then we won nine in a row before losing to Jordan again in the finals.

The experience was another reminder of how God was directing me in this particular phase of my life.

First, I enjoyed the teaching of Coach Mo, whether it was a multi-national morning Bible study with the competing teams' coaches or mentoring our own USA team.

Secondly, Coach Mo gave me the opportunity to share my testimony with our team, at the conclusion of which they all prayed over me. I had never been a part of something like that before.

Thirdly, I was able to travel somewhere special with Claudia for the first time in five years. Although we played games for ten days in a row, we had the last two days free to do some sightseeing.

Over the years, Claudia and I had been great travelers with our kids. Wherever we would go on vacation in August, Claudia would check ahead and plan interesting side trips we could take. And since we always took our kids to the NCAA tournaments, we saw some great points of interest in Washington D.C., Tucson, Sacramento, and Denver. In Taiwan, we saw the Chaing Kai-shek Memorial Hall and the Taipei 101, which at the time was one of the tallest buildings in the world. It was a lot of fun. We had some laughs for the first time in a long while. I had missed those laughs.

Thank you, Lord.

As Claudia and I returned from Taiwan to Texas, I decided to start a coaches' ministry that I called Game Plan Ministries. I had been contemplating this for several years, and my goal was to visit young coaches around the state to encourage them. On each visit, a coach might have me talk to his team or help with their practices. I also gave clinics around the state. The basis of every talk I gave was God's faithfulness, forgiveness, and hope. I would joke with coaches that my real purpose was to be a "traveling backrub" for them in order to encourage them to remember that coaching was actually a ministry. And although the ministry was meant to help high school coaches, especially the younger ones, it helped me the most.

Through all this, I was learning how valuable a comeback story can be—not just for you, but for others, too. What a radical concept it was for me to realize that someone else might benefit from my story. It almost seemed as if people could identify more with my failures than they ever did with my successes. I was learning that oftentimes this is how the gospel is best presented—through our weaknesses and through our shortcomings because this is where grace flourishes.

Author Tim Storey's book, *It's Time for Your Comeback*, helped me understand that, no matter what has happened in our lives up to a certain point, our lives can still have purpose and assignment. We were created to live by design, not by default.

I was learning that my situation and limitations didn't intimidate God; He can work with any mess and turn it into a message. It has nothing to do with our own abilities because when we are weak, God is strong. Jesus came back and conquered death, and the same Spirit that raised Him from the dead also lives in those who follow him. Why do we live "defeated lives" when this type of power dwells within us?

One Sunday, I was in church and the pastor's sermon brought everything full circle for me. He said that when tough things happen to people, we have a choice. We can live "defeated lives" and lay down, or we can fight back and show our faith in God. He went on to say that God was still in the miracle business and that we shouldn't let the fear of our circumstances blind us to His supernatural solutions. He closed with the admonition that, "We as believers need to stand for Jesus at a time when the world is standing for everything else."

I never could have imagined God's making good out of my wrongdoing. But as 1 Corinthians 15:10 (NASB) says, "By the grace of God, I am what I am, and His grace toward me did not prove vain, but I labored even more than all of them, yet not I, but the grace of God with me."

This comeback was about becoming the man that God had created me to be in the first place. My role was to obey God and accept His nurturing.

Just as I identified much with David and Peter as I sought forgiveness for my sins, the story of Nebuchadnezzar resonated with me throughout this whole "comeback" phase of my life.

Nebuchadnezzar was another king whose pride led to humiliation. His power led to pride, his pride led to a loss of perspective, and this led to impugning what was most true of him, the fact he was loved by God.

God, in His grace, even gave Nebuchadnezzar a dream to warn him that he had lost his way—a dream about a giant tree reaching into the heavens that was oddly similar to the Tower of Babel, visible to all, only to be chopped down. God even gave Nebuchadnezzar an interpreter of his dream, Daniel, who told him that the tree in his dream was a symbol of what Nebuchadnezzar had become; Daniel also warned Nebuchadnezzar that he, too, would be chopped down if he continued living in ignorance of the Almighty.

Similarly, God gave me several warnings and opportunities at Baylor to admit my wrongdoing and turn my life around. But I kept lying—my pride reigned—and the tree kept sprouting higher and higher.

Scriptures tell us that twelve months passed, and King Nebuchadnezzar still had not recognized that God was supreme; he was unchanged. We both remained on our thrones, believing we could do whatever we wanted.

That's when the dream Daniel interpreted came true. Nebuchadnezzar, whose hubris led to the belief that he was the center of the world, experienced a meteoric fall—from the life of a king to life like an animal, banished from his people and reduced to eating grass like an ox—a reminder from God that he was merely a man.

I, too, endured a meteoric fall and felt as if I had been banished from my people, no longer able to coach and encourage kids as I had done for my entire life.

But there is hope for Nebuchadnezzar in Daniel 4:36-37 (ESV):

At the same time my reason returned to me, and for the glory of my kingdom, my majesty and splendor returned to me. My counselors and my lords sought me, and I was established in my kingdom, and still more greatness was added to me. Now I, Nebuchadnezzar, praise and extol and honor the King of heaven, for all his works are right and his ways are just; and those who walk in pride he is able to humble.

I love that the Scriptures say Nebuchadnezzar's "reason" returned to him. His very identity, his self-esteem—all based on the foundation of God's love and grace—all were restored once He looked up to the heavens to acknowledge the Author of Life.

I did not know it yet, but much like King Nebuchadnezzar, I would see my "reason" returned to me in my seventh year after the scandal, just like his seven periods of time that elapsed for him.

God would put my piece back on the board—the coaching board.

RESTORED

"You will seek me and find me when you seek me with all your heart. I will be found by you," declares the Lord, "and will bring you back from captivity. I will gather you from all the nations and places where I have banished you," declares the Lord, "and will bring you back to the place from which I carried you into exile."

Jeremiah 29:13-14 (NIV)

It seemed to me that any comeback journey starts by making the decision that what you have lost is worth regaining.

Although I knew that Claudia's and my life, as it existed before, was over, I refused to accept that something good couldn't evolve during the time we had left. I realized how much I had disappointed her and let her down when she needed me most, but I wanted to try and "finish strong," whatever that included. She deserved more, but I was determined to try my best, and I prayed that God would help us.

With my career, I now believed that the authenticity of my comeback would depend on my desire to allow God to accomplish His goal with my life. My clay vessel might continue to be put through the fire—I knew there would be resistance because resistance is a part of life—but I was committed not to quit on

Him. And whereas some people might resent any thought of a basketball comeback for me, that wasn't what my comeback was about anymore.

I was discovering that the best thing about coming before God in brokenness and surrender is that words like "difficult" and "hard" became irrelevant when a comeback is God-centered. I felt free in His will. I stopped telling God how big my mountains were and started telling my mountains how big God was, as I heard a pastor once say. This allowed me to enjoy the experience of depending on God as He took over the controls of my life.

By 2009, I had an unusual feeling that once God thought my priorities were back in order, He might allow me to do what I loved again: coach basketball. I felt a heavy restlessness to return to the coaching ranks. God had taken my playing piece off the board a half-dozen years before, but that was so He could work me through the re-development of my purpose—I felt like a brand new person.

Still, for the next eleven months, nothing significant surfaced on the job front. In the meantime, I took a part-time job working as an assistant in the golf shop at Plum Creek Golf Course near my home.

Late in the spring of 2010, however, it looked like there might be something available when the head coach at Hays High School in Kyle, Texas, left for another job. During the previous season, I had spent some time with the head coach and his team, so I knew the players pretty well. As a result, several of the parents urged me to apply. It seemed like a perfect fit as the school was less than a mile from where Claudia and I were living. At the same time, I also had applied for several other public high school basketball jobs within a thirty-mile radius of our home.

But I didn't get the Hays job.

Nor any of the other jobs I applied for.

Truth is, I really wanted the Hays job and was extremely discouraged when it was apparent that the lack of my teaching credentials was preventing me from getting the positions. Three and a half decades of coaching experience wasn't enough.

Would I ever be able to coach again?

I was not any good at waiting—it was not in my DNA. Waiting, to me, always implied not being aggressive, and I had been trained to be aggressive. But now I was learning that the "waiting room" of faith was an opportunity for me to show God how I had changed. And if I had truly changed, I needed to reflect what God knew was on my heart. I started praying intently about another opportunity in coaching, and I focused on the fact that I would not abuse my next opportunity. I asked Him to direct me to the place where He needed me most . . . and then I waited . . . and waited some more.

Two more months went by.

As I prayed that the right job might surface, I also changed my approach. If I was being told that I didn't have the proper teaching credentials for a public school position, perhaps I should either get the credentials or look at private schools because they weren't as demanding of these credentials. Since going back to school seemed out of the question, I pursued the private school option.

In an effort to find a private school opportunity, I went online and looked around at the various postings. After checking for several days, I stumbled upon an understated post on the Texas Association of Private and Parochial Schools (TAPPS) site that seemed to be tailor-made for my experience and abilities. It read, very simply, that there was a position open for:

Allen Academy
Dean of Students and Athletic Director
Bryan, Texas

I had been to the Bryan/College Station area numerous times before when my teams would compete against Texas A&M, but I had never heard of Allen Academy. I went online and investigated. It claimed to be the oldest college preparatory school in Texas, and it looked pretty interesting.

I was to attend a coaching clinic in Nacogdoches, Texas, that weekend, so I looked at the map to see where Allen Academy was located. Surprisingly, I discovered that on my way to the clinic, I would drive right by Allen Academy on State Highway 21. This is the state of Texas, remember, practically a country in itself, so when I saw I was going directly past the school, I thought it rather curious.

On that Friday, I left a little early for the clinic so I could swing by the school. It was probably a long shot, but I wanted to check the school out. As I drove into Bryan, I took a right on Boonville Road and drove through town. On the south side of town, there in the distance, was Allen Academy.

The campus appeared impressive as I turned left to enter in through the stately front gates. Immediately, I saw a long, stone wall dominated by gigantic black lettering reading "Allen Academy" highlighted by the glow of spotlights. The lawn beyond the wall led up to what I imagined was their main academic building. The building was beautiful, built in red and beige brick, divided by a roofed courtyard with four towering pillars. It looked like how I envisioned a private school should look.

I parked my car in the lot adjacent to the main building and walked up the path that led to the campus. As I was walking, I noticed how well-kept everything was—beautiful buildings, trimmed landscape, and colorful flowerbeds. Then I circled around the grounds until I came to the athletic fields. I could see the turf football field in the distance, an impressive gym, and a freshly-mowed baseball field. Although everything was locked for the evening, I took note of the more-than-adequate facilities.

Over the years, whenever I would job-hunt at different schools, I had developed the ability to get a good "first blush" feeling of sorts, as to whether or not a school would be a good fit. I became somewhat adept at discerning whether it would be a good place at which to work.

As I walked back down the path toward my car, I felt tremendous anxiety.

On the one hand, the school had passed the "first blush" test with flying colors. But on the other hand, I tried not to get too excited because, if I thought the job was a good opportunity, I had to imagine everybody else probably thought so, too. And who was to say that the job hadn't already been filled? Plus, I had to face the fact that Allen Academy might not be interested in hiring a guy named Dave Bliss, the ex-Baylor coach. I knew the odds were against me.

Regardless, I felt impressed with everything about Allen Academy, and I got back in my car to continue my drive to Nacogdoches. I hadn't hit the road five minutes before I started to pray that Allen Academy might be just the opportunity I was looking for.

After the clinic on Saturday, I had a powerful urge to drive by Allen's campus again, so I did. I replicated the same process as on Friday and admitted to myself that, even though the odds were probably against me, I would do everything I could to get the position. Just like the old days, I decided I would put on the "full-court press." When I returned home, I told Claudia all about my trip. I am pretty sure she could sense I was excited, but, on the other hand, I hadn't been too successful in the job-searching lately.

Maybe this time would be different.

I spent the next day, Sunday morning, preparing my résumé to take to Allen. I had hardly touched my résumé in twenty years—I was fortunate enough to never have to. Most of my jobs following the scandal came through connections I had made in three decades of coaching.

On Monday morning I took my résumé and made the two-hour drive back over to Allen. I was determined. It seemed as if there was a gentle breeze behind me, encouraging me to take the next step.

Arriving shortly before noon, I left my résumé with a kind receptionist named Barbara—she told me that there was a bit of a hold-up in the AD job search because the new head of school was finishing up his previous job in Colorado.

I drove back home and told Claudia about my visit. She listened politely, then proceeded to ask me, "Did you fill out an application?"

"Nuts," I replied, "I didn't even think about that." So the next day I got back in the car and made the one hundred-mile drive to Bryan again—my fourth trip in five days—to deliver my application.

When I arrived at the school, I was determined to hand my application to a person. Right when I got there, Barbara grabbed me and pointed me toward two people who were talking together across the hall. Kathy Duewall, the interim head of school, and her husband, Chris, just happened to be walking out of a meeting. I had fortunately arrived at Allen right when the meeting ended. I waited until they had finished their conversation and walked over to introduce myself.

We exchanged hellos, and I was pleased that they seemed to be somewhat interested. They mentioned seeing my résumé, and, after some introductory comments, asked if I had time to visit with them a little further. I, of course, said yes and was ushered into a small conference room off the rotunda area. After about fifteen minutes of interviewing, they disappeared for a couple of minutes; I assumed to discuss my application. When they returned, it was determined that Chris and I would go out for lunch while Kathy set up some meetings for later that afternoon. The meetings were typical of several interview situations I had been in before, and I enjoyed learning about Allen. After talking with several faculty members and a board member, it was agreed that they would be in touch.

As I drove home, I was on cloud nine. I still recognized that I might not get the job, but it was apparent that the position was still open.

The following evening I received a call from the board chair at Allen, Jerry Bullin, about the prospect of flying to Colorado to meet the new head of school that Allen Academy had just hired: John Rouse.

Rouse.

The same last name as the coach who taped me apparently now held the keys to my second chance.

On top of that, the meeting would take place the following Monday in Colorado Springs, close to where Mr. Rouse was finishing his term as the superintendent at another school.

Colorado Springs.

The very place I started meeting with Gary Lydic, which began my process of recovery.

I am sure that Mr. Rouse had his own preconceived notions about me. When the administration heard of my interest, I'm guessing he immediately typed "Dave Bliss" into Google. I'm sure he saw that I was connected to the Baylor fiasco, and he probably noticed the negative phrases like "fall from grace" and "worst scandal in college basketball history."

He would have to be suspicious, and rightfully so. He had to wonder why a Division I coach would want to work at little Allen Academy. Everywhere I went from now on, I understood that I would carry the baggage of my past. This is the reality of the world we live in. Just because you are forgiven eternally does not mean you still may not pay earthly consequences.

But as I boarded a plane from Austin to Colorado Springs, I had a feeling that if things went okay, it might be the second chance I had been praying for.

Mr. Rouse met me at the airport. Not long after we shook hands, I was already launching into my story as it was certainly the elephant in the room. Why avoid it? Interestingly enough, he seemed strangely connected to my story, and I think he was somewhat surprised.

He told me he was looking for an athletic director who wanted to be at Allen Academy primarily to help the children—whether that was through sports or simple day-to-day encouragement or discipline. I told him that was exactly why I wanted the job—because of the opportunity to work with young people again. He asked how long I thought I would want to work at Allen and if I wanted to get involved in professional basketball or something that was more in the limelight. I told him that I was more interested in the position at Allen Academy than coaching in the pros. I concluded by telling him that my passions had been redirected and I was excited to return to the reason I entered coaching to begin with—to get young people excited about who and what they could become.

After our visit in Colorado Springs, Mr. Rouse continued his research. He called former Baylor University president Robert Sloan, and Mr. Sloan spoke openly and honestly to Mr. Rouse about the happenings at Baylor and our relationship.

Somehow, some way, Mr. Rouse decided he would take a chance on me.

Mr. Rouse called the Allen administration and told them he wanted to hire me. He believed I could help build Allen's athletic program. I would also be coaching their basketball team. Considering my hiring was one of his first moves as the new head of school, it was a pretty bold move, especially given that Baylor University is less than an hour and a half straight up Highway 6 from Bryan, Texas.

And similar to Athletes In Action's decision to have me speak at the Final Four, Mr. Rouse also experienced resistance with the hire. A news article reported that several families withdrew their children from the school, although they left before I got the job. Local and national journalists contacted Mr. Rouse for comments.

I appreciated that Mr. Rouse and the others weren't bothered by any of it. They all supported me, and so did a lot of the parents. In a *USA Today* article, Mr. Rouse was quoted saying, "I believe

in forgiveness and the chance to give somebody a second chance."
Thank you, God.

I definitely considered Allen Academy my second chance. I was determined to make it work, not only for me, but for all the others down the line who also might deserve a second chance. I was, in fact, the poster child for second chances. Early in my first year at Allen, however, we faced a situation that made me aware of the scrutiny that I would be under, probably for the rest of my life.

Upon taking the Allen position in early May 2010, my hire was given a great deal of publicity throughout the country. As the word spread, I was besieged by phone calls from coaches and parents asking about our basketball program which I would be coaching. I had inquiries from representatives of players from Russia, Spain, Australia, the Bahamas, Canada, and Cameroon. They all wanted to know if the oldest college prep school in the state of Texas had designs on creating a basketball powerhouse because if we were, they had players they wanted to send to us.

I quickly related that Allen Academy was a great academic school, which hired me to upgrade their athletic programs. They wanted an athletic program that would take advantage of their outstanding facilities.

Months before they hired me, Allen had also re-established itself as a boarding school and rented out a section of apartments near Texas A&M. These apartments mainly housed our international students, mostly from China, but this housing would technically be available to anyone who wanted to attend the school. The governing organization Texas Association of Private and Parochial Schools (TAPPS) was afraid that Allen was going to follow the example of a school in San Antonio who, fifteen years prior, had used their boarding house to field an all-star team from Mexico. That wasn't what we were doing, but TAPPS, nonetheless, became suspicious. They were convinced that we were going to become a basketball factory.

A couple of weeks went by and during this period, two student-athletes from Houston applied to Allen and were accepted. Both were young African-Americans, and although both were very good at basketball, they were even better students. They both indicated that they were not returning to their previous school, so we were glad they wanted to attend Allen. They also applied for and received tuition remission, the same assistance available to all families. TAPPS heard about the transfers from some parents and jilted coaches and asked us to come down to Salado, Texas—home to TAPPS—to state our intentions. Before we went down, I asked TAPPS to list their concerns so we could be prepared at the meeting.

When the day of the meeting arrived, John Rouse and I took the two families with us down to Salado. We were prepared to answer their concerns, but the meeting immediately turned into World War III. We walked into a room full of skeptical administrators who never even looked at the report we had prepared. Not one page.

I think it had finally occurred to them that we had done nothing wrong, but during the cross-examination they came upon the fact that I had "forged" Mr. Rouse's signature to a transfer form of another young man who never attended Allen. I had done it innocently, as it was just a clerical signature, because there had been a time crunch and I was trying to help the student who was more interested in music than sports get in under the wire. But this showed me that I needed to be very cautious in everything I did from now on because my actions would be scrutinized. Above all, I didn't want to let the Allen people down.

Because of the signature mistake, TAPPS placed Allen on two years of probation and suspended me for a year. Allen disputed the severity of the penalty which I appreciated, but it was my fault—I had to be more careful. In a show of support, Mr. Rouse and the Board of Trustees decided to pull out of TAPPS and immediately join the Texas Christian Athletic League, which was actually a better fit for our small school. Though we were not a Christian school, Allen Academy's values and principles lined up with the other schools in the conference.

Mr. Rouse was quoted saying this about TAPPS: "My belief is they are a bunch of self-pious individuals out to pass judgment on people." Even some of the newspaper articles recognized that there might be extra scrutiny where I was involved.

This was a great example to me that from now on, I had to be wary of doing anything that jeopardized my witness because I was easy pickings for anyone who needed a news article.

In *The Purpose Driven Life*, Rick Warren says that, "endurance develops every time you reject the temptation to give up." Each time my past seemed to arise, I would be tempted to return to the same enslaving guilt that paralyzed me from experiencing purpose for years. My guilt took me to a dark place, like my long nights in Waco or those snowy days in Denver. But Warren says this in Chapter 25 of his best-seller:

> *It is vital that you stay focused on God's plan, not your pain or problem . . . Corrie ten Boom, who suffered in a Nazi death camp, explained the power of focus: "If you look at the world, you'll be distressed. If you look within, you'll be depressed. But if you look at Christ, you'll be at rest!" Your focus will determine your feelings. The secret of endurance is to remember that your pain is temporary but your reward will be eternal.*

I will always be thankful for the chance Mr. Rouse took with hiring me, his support in the TAPPS dilemma, and the confidence he instilled in me. Allen was right where I needed to be, and I felt it was where God wanted me. It was my second chance and an opportunity to hopefully impact kids again through athletics. I was back doing something that aligned with the passions and gifts God had given me. I couldn't have been more grateful.

⁊

One morning, I was taking a walk around my neighborhood, as I did most mornings after my quiet time with God. I happened to be wearing a University of Arizona T-shirt (in honor of our two sons' undergraduate degrees), and as I was walking around the bend in the road, I passed by a couple who were busy chatting with each other, headed in the opposite direction.

We exchanged polite hellos, passed one another, and continued walking in our opposite directions.

Then, a second later, I heard the man's voice from behind me. "Hey!" he yelled.

I turned around.

"I've got some extra tickets to the Texas A&M and Arizona baseball game this afternoon, if you'd like to go," the husband offered. I figured he must have noticed my Arizona T-shirt.

"That would be great. I'd love to go," I told him. "By the way, I'm Dave Bliss," I said, holding out my hand.

"I'm George Boykin," the husband said. "And this is my wife, Bonny. Do you live around here?"

"I live in that duplex right over there," I said, pointing down the street toward a row of houses. I had been renting the dwelling since getting the Allen position several months prior.

"Well, we live right over there," he said, motioning to a red, brick two-story house a block away. "Come on and walk with us, and then I'll get the tickets for you," George told me.

I changed directions and as we continued our walk together, he asked what I did. I said that I was the director of athletics at Allen Academy, and I saw his eyes light up. He seemed very intrigued with Allen Academy for some reason.

As our walk continued, he told me a story about an eleven-year-old boy named Steven who was the grandchild of a woman who had helped around George and Bonny's house for several years. Steven lived with his grandmother and was attending a local elementary school, but George had been thinking about Steven attending Allen for several months. George also said that although

Steven was only in the sixth grade, he was shaping up to be one heck of a basketball player.

"Allen has a basketball team, don't they?" George asked me.

"Absolutely," I told him.

I went on to tell George more about Allen Academy. I hadn't been there very long, but my assessment of Allen during my initial walk around the grounds a year prior had only been enhanced when I got to know the people who worked there. Obviously, I had never worked at a high school, much less a private school, but I hadn't been around too many places where all the people valued the children like they did at Allen. The teachers were amazing in their dedication and commitment to their young students, and it seemed that many of them were qualified to be teachers at a much higher level than Allen. The class sizes were small, allowing the teachers to really educate the kids.

At the conclusion of each day, I thanked God for directing me to such a wonderful place. My second chance was working out far beyond my wildest expectations. I felt that Allen would be a great place for almost anyone, but certainly a young man like Steven.

As I followed them into the house to get the tickets, I noticed a photograph on their refrigerator of a young African-American boy with a contagious smile. I wondered if this was Steven.

"Is this him?" I asked George.

"Yep, that's him," George smiled. I could tell that Steven was very important to George.

"With a smile like that, he'll do just fine at Allen," I assured him.

That was the start of my friendship with George and Bonny, but also the start of my friendship with Steven. Steven's road to Allen Academy began that fall, and each day, as I walked through the halls and saw Steven's smile, I knew I was exactly where God wanted me to be. Steven was a reminder to me that God uses improbable, unplanned circumstances—like an early morning walk around the neighborhood—to accomplish His purposes and meet the needs of a people He loves.

Steven was also a daily reminder to me that the obstacles and pain endured on my comeback journey were being eased by the joy and purpose that I was gaining from trying to impact a young man's life in a positive manner.

At Allen Academy, not only did I feel that my purpose had been restored, but I also felt my self-esteem was being restored.

After Baylor, the thought of never being able to feel good about myself again was terribly depressing. It did not resonate with what I remember having learned in my Psychology 101 class at Cornell. Abraham Maslow, an American psychologist, included self-esteem in his hierarchy of human needs and described two forms of esteem needs: the need for respect from others, and the need for self-respect and esteem from within. For the longest time, I had neither.

I discovered that there was nothing that I could do to work my way back into the good favor of the world; no amount of interviews or television appearances would restore my shattered self-esteem. I felt empty and incapable of doing much of anything. It appeared that I would have to spend the rest of my life incapable of ever reclaiming my self-esteem.

As I was working my way back in my God-discovery, however, I uncovered two important principles that renewed my hope. First, I learned that God gave me my capability (gifts) at birth; and second, He qualified my emotional needs at the cross. As I looked back, most of my career was spent just "striving after the wind" because I never gave God enough credit on the front side for supplying my "gifts" (arrogance), nor did I realize that Jesus' death on the cross qualified my emotional needs (ignorance).

I now experienced that the true harmony in a man's life seems to be based on how well he can stay in rhythm with what God's purpose is for him. Sin and guilt, however, constantly interrupt this rhythm.

Although my sin may have changed the plans for my life, it didn't

affect God's purpose for my life.

I can't tell you how this simple revelation helped restore my self-esteem. It gave me tremendous hope that I could bounce back because He still had a purpose for me, despite my brokenness.

What I found amazing was that once I received the opportunity at Allen Academy, my life seemed to "click back" into place. Although I couldn't explain it at the time, it seemed as if my entire existence reverted back into complete harmony with God's purpose for my life.

At Allen Academy, I was back in coaching, using the talents that God had gifted me with, and I was also now emotionally stable because I knew I was operating within the purpose of God's plan. Allen Academy was where God wanted me.

I believe God orchestrated everything in my return to coaching at Allen. I believe He placed the advertisement on the TAPPS website that no one else saw; I believe He planned the clinic to be on the same road as Allen; I believe He involved some terrific people at Allen to aid in my hiring; and I believe He continues to work with my clay to this day.

Like King Nebuchadnezzar, it was as if my reason had finally returned. It had taken Nebuchadnezzar seven long years and almost the same in my own life. Just as Rick Warren had written—my comeback was not what I expected, but I was grateful that He had "restored" me, and I would do everything I could to justify His faith in me.

26

SERVICE

Within weeks of my resignation at Baylor in 2003, I received a letter from the senior manager of my Cornell basketball team, Hugh Snyder, Class of '65. His letter was a soothing reminder that my friends hadn't all forgotten me, although I hadn't conversed with Hugh since graduating, almost forty years prior.

He related to me that for the past nine years he had been coping with a spinal cord condition known as syringomyelia, the same condition that golfing legend Bobby Jones had contracted. Hugh went on to share that, although he had four surgeries and numerous trips to a rehabilitative hospital, he had unfortunately also witnessed several patients in more dire conditions than his.

His two-page letter encouraged me in several areas.

First of all, he encouraged me to see the larger perspective—that we live in a fallen world and things happen, dreadful things, and we shouldn't succumb to the world's pity party. He mentioned that "the same Dave Bliss who had valiantly scored twenty-eight points in a losing effort to Princeton in his final college game, was the same Dave Bliss who wouldn't quit now."

He also suggested that I do acts of intrinsic kindness for someone with no consideration given to them having to repay the favor. He mentioned others like Chuck Colson who had lost their moral compass but "took stock of themselves and acted in positive ways to contribute to the betterment of their communities." He closed with this:

Doing things which bring you a sense of contribution are

their own reward and provide a counterweight to the current circumstances you find yourself in. Focusing on doing good works in the future, while not avoiding the responsibility for those actions you regret engaging in, would seem to be one way to move forward. While not discounting the difficulties you will face in doing this, and the painful change involved, I have no doubt that you have the ability to do that. I wish you well in that effort.

When I read that letter in my depths, I remember appreciating that Hugh thought enough to write me at this terrible juncture of my life, but I had no idea how to use this seemingly valuable advice because I was in such shock—especially the part about helping others. I couldn't begin to think about others because I was in a seemingly timeless free fall. I do remember being impacted, however, by the thought that although I was at the lowest ebb of my life and everything was cascading down upon me, he admonished me to think beyond myself, to serve someone else. Because I was in such a bad mental state, I didn't know to implement this then, but more than a decade later, I remembered his letter and pulled it out.

Doing things for others seemed to be exactly where I needed to be in my life. It actually kept me from thinking about my past, and, for perhaps the first time in my life, I understood what it meant to serve others by allowing God to work through me.

For whatever reason, I had no desire to return to my former life of elevating myself every chance I got. Quite the contrary, doing something for others now provided a whole different level of satisfaction. This desire to help others gave me a tremendous boost toward restoring my important God-centered self-esteem.

And whereas before, I would serve others in an attempt to please God and continue to earn my "Get Into Heaven Free" card, now I was allowing God to direct my steps in order to serve others through me with the time I had here on this earth.

I once heard it said that no matter what has occurred before, we all have opportunities to become trophies of grace. I do not remember who said it, but I believe it is true of everyone. If we are to believe Romans in the Bible, which I do, we have all stumbled. We all have a story where we have chosen our own ways and pursued Bathsheba over God's ways. And we all must come to grips with the repentance King David expresses in Psalm 51.

Though my story is unique in the sense that my life unraveled for the entire world to see, I believe ultimately we all must arrive at the conclusion that we are hopeless without accepting God's grace. We all need saving. We all must come back. We all need restoring. And we must do it time and time again.

Author Brennan Manning says this about the apostles in his book *The Ragamuffin Gospel:*

> One morning at prayer, I heard this word—"Little brother, I witnessed a Peter who claimed that he did not know Me, a James who wanted power in return for service to the kingdom, a Philip who failed to see the Father in Me, and scores of disciples who were convinced I was finished on Calvary. The New Testament has many examples of men and women who started out well and then faltered along the way. Yet on Easter night I appeared to Peter. James is not remembered for his ambition but for the sacrifice of his life for Me. Philip did see the Father in Me when I pointed the way, and the disciples who despaired had enough courage to recognize Me when we broke bread at the end of the road to Emmaus. My point, little brother, is this—I expect more failure from you than you expect from yourself."

After my coaching career unraveled, I came face-to-face with a number of questions: What do I do next? Do I return to a life dependent on works, or do I adopt the gospel of faith? Do I accept the grace I read about in the Bible, or will I, as Brennan Manning says in *The Ragamuffin Gospel*, continue to "apply spiritual cosmetics to make myself presentable"? Will I continue to live in ignorance?

Grace was proving to be a very difficult thing to accept.

And as I worked through my issues, I discovered that understanding and accepting grace is the key that unlocked all of my chains and allowed me to run freely toward something better, a life more fulfilling, a life the way it was designed by the Designer.

Grace is the only means that allowed me to forget what is behind and strain toward what is ahead, as Paul says in Philippians 3:13. Manning, perhaps, understood this better than anyone because of his own sin and battle with alcoholism. He continues in *The Ragamuffin Gospel:*

> *Whatever past achievements might bring us honor, whatever past disgraces might make us blush, all have been crucified with Christ and exist no more except in the deep recesses of eternity, where "good is enhanced into glory and evil is miraculously established as part of a greater good."*

I have come to the realization that perhaps all of life flows from grace. All the headlines may have shouted that I "fell from grace," but the reality is that, thankfully, I "fell to grace" instead—and it caught me like the safety net it is.

I received letters from my friends during the free fall, and they were glimpses of something beautiful, an affirmation that I did not quite yet understand; a glimmer of hope at a time when I had none; it was grace because God met me right where I was, and He did not have to.

But I did not understand this thing called grace.

Grace ensued, as I hit rock bottom. Lifeless after the fall, God performed His autopsy on me, examining my heart and soul and mind, and then rewiring me so He would be my strength. It was His grace that broke me, and He did not have to. It was His grace that chastened me, and He did not have to.

But I still did not understand.

Grace ensued, as His love brought me to life again, and I gradually awakened to an identity as His child. Though I looked in the mirror each day and saw a man of whom I was not proud, God saw something different. My own perception of myself was not my reality and others' perceptions of me were not reality, but rather His unconditional love for me was reality. I was His; and He was mine, if I was man enough to accept Him. It was His grace that breathed renewed hope into me, and He did not have to.

But I still did not understand.

Grace ensued, and He taught me about renewed purpose and complete restoration because I was a new creation, because I was now His, and He not only gave me new life, but He also forgave the old, and He did not have to. It was grace because He brought meaning and purpose back into my life, and He did not have to.

But I still did not understand.

Grace ensued, and it still ensues, as I learn more every day about a God who sent His Son to die for us, the greatest demonstration of love and grace ever known; then rose from the dead, the greatest demonstration of hope and promise ever shown; then unleashed His Spirit to live in us and through us, the greatest demonstration of purpose and joy ever sown; its ultimate purpose—to help us prepare for life eternal.

And I must confess: I may not ever fully understand this thing called grace.

Grace calls us to service because grace changes our thinking.

It comes without bondage because it wipes away the sins of our pasts, but believing in something that magnificent must radically change our futures. Dietrich Bonhoeffer, a German theologian and Christian martyr in Nazi Germany, would put it this way in his book *The Cost of Discipleship*: "The only man who has the right to say that he is justified by grace alone is the man who left all to follow Christ."

God's unwavering love is such an unfathomable gift that the only response has to be obedience. It's a "costly grace," as Bonhoeffer calls it, for it cost God His very Son, and it's a grace that demands my life and all. But if God is the foundation of life— if the purpose of our existence is to glorify Him and enjoy Him throughout all of eternity—then living for something other than Him, as I did for much of my life, is selling ourselves drastically short of true meaning and purpose.

My supreme goal in life, now, is simply to pursue and enjoy God.

I don't have to prove my worth anymore because now I live for an eternal God who has redeemed my troubled past and turned it into a trophy of grace, echoing the words of John Newton's famous hymn:

Amazing Grace, how sweet the sound,
That saved a wretch like me.
I once was lost but now am found,
Was blind, but now I see.

'Twas Grace that taught my heart to fear.
And Grace, my fears relieved.
How precious did that Grace appear
The hour I first believed.

Through many dangers, toils and snares
I have already come;
'Tis Grace that brought me safe thus far
and Grace will lead me home.

The Lord has promised good to me.
His word my hope secures.
He will my shield and portion be,
As long as life endures.

Yea, when this flesh and heart shall fail,
And mortal life shall cease,
I shall possess within the veil,
A life of joy and peace. . . .

And now, because I trust God implicitly with the remainder of my life, His grace has come full circle.

My supreme goal in life, now, is simply to pursue and enjoy God.

27

THE CALM

"A life of joy and peace," the last line in John Newton's hymn, is another byproduct of this amazing grace. Maybe Newton ends on that line for a reason—because that is what grace tangibly does best, and maybe because peace is what we all want most, even though we may not realize what it really is or how much it adds to our life.

As I look back, this is what my three decades of coaching can be summarized as—striving after peace. I felt purpose much of the time because I was coaching. I experienced happiness some of the time because we were winning. But, as I look back, I'm not sure I ever had any peace because a performance-driven person always creates more to do.

The success was never enough. The wins were never enough. Rings, watches, trophies, five hundred victories—whatever it was—just didn't do it for me. Or else I don't think I would have cheated. There was always more to do, always better players we needed to get, and better seasons to have. It became obvious that the world and all my ambition only created the desire for more—making peace unobtainable.

But it was not the world's fault; it was my view of the world and my view of God in the context of that world. My faulty metaphor for God—an impersonal, distant, Straitjacket Santa Claus—allowed my heart, mind, and soul to elevate the world more than I should have.

As I've said, I believed I was a Christian all along; I just did not know how much God loved me. For many, and for myself, it was not a categorical issue—Christian or non-Christian, believer or non-believer—it was one of theology, how big you believe God to be, and how small you think He can be.

I did not know how much God loved me until I was broken, and His love ultimately brought me to surrender. This brought transcending peace—peace because Someone else's opinion of me was greater than my own (self-esteem), Someone else's direction was greater than my wandering (purpose), and, frankly, if there was Someone out there willing to save me for all of eternity, then that Someone would surely live through my broken life here on earth (self-esteem with purpose).

The whole message of the gospel, from Jesus coming into this world as an infant and eventually dying as an accused criminal, is that God is with the broken. And I was now believing that my life is a testament to that, for I was lost 'til grace found me, blind 'til it helped me see, and ignorant 'til I was comforted by a love so strong. And grace will surely lead me home.

In *The Purpose Driven Life*, Rick Warren says that knowing your purpose will simplify your life:

> *Without a clear purpose you have no foundation on which you base decisions, allocate your time, and use your resources. You will tend to make choices based on circumstances, pressures, and your mood at the moment. People who don't know their purposes try to do too much—and that causes stress, fatigue, and conflict.*

This was certainly true in my own life. I had a faulty foundation, and I decided to pay the scholarships because I allowed my circumstances, pressures, and mood to rule me. Circumstances and pressures come from a fallen world, and our mood and emotions come from our fallen selves, so if these things dictate how we act in absence of a firm foundation, our lives will surely destruct and result in sin. And trust me, "destruct" is the nicest word that can be used to describe what my life became.

I love the words of Isaiah 26:3 (GNT): "You, Lord, give perfect peace to those who keep their purposes firm and put their trust in you." Think about that. Perfect peace. If the world will never satisfy, then perfect peace must come from something else. And that something else, I believe, is a relationship with Jesus Christ. I tried to find it in the world. Until the fall, I had a career many people might dream of having. But I was never really at peace.

The whirlwind has passed, however, and now I experience the calm.

Each day is an opportunity for me to experience the peace and purpose Isaiah 26:3 talks about. I believe the Lord has constructed my comeback and handcrafted each step along the way. I think He molded me for a comeback, and I believe He will continue molding me through the things He places before me. I have not arrived, for He continues to do a work in me, but I have learned how to experience peace in the journey.

God has allowed Allen Academy to help me get some spring back in my step again. I really enjoy the people. I value the kids and love the job, no matter what task I'm completing—whether it's coaching a varsity basketball practice, refereeing a middle school volleyball game, or delivering the announcements to students during their free period.

Through Allen Academy, God has flipped my world back to right-side up. Everything I experienced as a head coach at the Division I level—the awards, the victories, the trophies, the fame—seem to be in the rear-view mirror now that I am at Allen Academy. Whether I am folding up tables after a banquet or counseling a youngster about the value of self-control, Allen Academy is an opportunity for me to do what God created me to do: encourage young people.

I don't have to "feed the dragon" anymore, so to speak. Sure, I don't have my great college job back, but that obviously hadn't given me peace. I can go to work every day and have a positive, unadulterated confidence as I try to have an impact on kids' lives again. I can hug a kid simply because I care about him, not because I'm trying to play a mind game with him so he scores twenty points against Arizona. I can discipline a kid because I know it's best for him, not because I'm trying to get him eligible for the NCAA tournament. As Proverbs 13:7 (The Message) says, "A pretentious, showy life is an empty life; a plain and simple life is a full life."

When my life fell apart, I had no idea what to do with the fact that my identity had been stripped away from me. But striving after the impossible is not who I am anymore; my entire focus is on accomplishing God's will for my life and this has given me the freedom of knowing who I am.

Finally, there is peace.

Theologian Charles Spurgeon says that Psalm 51, David's song of repentance after Nathan confronted him about Bathsheba, may be "the most plaintive" of all the Psalms; but Psalm 84, Spurgeon says, is "most sweet of the Psalms of peace."

> *How lovely is your dwelling place*
> *Lord Almighty!*
> *My soul yearns, even faints,*
> *for the courts of the Lord;*
> *my heart and my flesh cry out*
> *for the living God.*
>
> *Psalm 84:1-2*

In awakening to my new identity as one who is loved by God, experiencing Him and being obedient to Him became the most important thing in my life. Pursuing the things of the world no longer mattered as much because of the values that the Creator of this world awakened in me. A God who, in my ignorance, I believed was distant was now living within me and through me. And whenever we realize that the One who created the universe is living within us, we experience an unbelievable peace because of the confidence of knowing that His hand is in our lives. This newfound presence brought me peace.

I had spent so much of my life chasing the wind, trying to accumulate things that I cannot take to my grave, while the only thing that extends into eternity is the fact that, as David says in Psalm 84:4, we will ever be praising God. And this eternal reality made me want to praise and live for Him on earth. This lasting purpose brought me peace.

God became my strength. And His strength was in me (Psalm 84:5). My whole life, I had been in a state of discontent because I could never accomplish enough. But now, as Spurgeon says, "When we have God's ways in our hearts, and our heart in His ways, we are what and where we should be, and hence we shall enjoy the divine approval." I found contentment in knowing I was right where He wanted me—even if it was not as flashy in the world's eyes—and this brought me peace.

After my free fall, autopsy, and wilderness, I lifted my eyes to heaven and learned that my strength and growth in the Lord was a process of endless discovery and wonder. I could tell that things were changing within me and this brought me peace.

I never envisioned my legacy being what it had become. As I shared my broken story and how God had rescued me with His grace, I was reminded of what Henri Nouwen says in his book, *Life of the Beloved:* "I never realized that broken glass could shine so brightly." I was starting to believe He could do something good with my broken life. It all brought me peace I had never experienced before.

> *For the Lord God is a sun and shield;*
> *the Lord bestows favor and honor;*
> *no good thing does he withhold*
> *from those whose walk is blameless*
> *Lord Almighty,*
> *blessed is the one who trusts in you.*
>
> *Psalm 84:11-12*

Now, finally, I understood that God truly loved me. And this brought me peace. I felt more "favor and honor" than ever before, even if it was undeserved. This grace that I now experienced saved me and this same grace was changing me. I was loved, and I would forever give God my all, in exploration of this amazing reality.

EPILOGUE

In the summer of 2014, our family spent five days together in a rented beach house on Galveston Island. It was a wonderful time as we shared in each other's lives for the first time in a few years. There is no doubt that the little people (grandchildren) made it even more fun.

The time went way too fast, but it was a wonderful occasion. As we all finished packing for the return to our various lives—Jeff back to California; Rob, his wife, Laura, and their children, Caroline and Anna, back to Denver; Berkeley, her husband, James, and their children, Brynn and Owen, back to Austin; and Claudia and I back to Austin (where we have a house)—I asked them all to meet me in the large family room.

As they filed in, not knowing what it was all about, I told them that I wanted to say a prayer. In the first part of the prayer, I thanked God for the wonderful time we had and prayed that we would be safe until we were together again. In closing the prayer, I thanked God for blessing me with such a remarkable family—I loved each one of them, and although we had been through an awful lot together and had been tested to the hilt, by God's grace, we were survivors.

The person for whom I am most grateful is the architect of our family's endurance: our children's mother, Claudia.

For twenty-five years, similar to a lot of coaches' wives, Claudia operated behind the scenes and out of the spotlight. As I have said before, she was the consummate coach's wife. Over the years, she did everything she could to make our players feel genuinely welcome and looked after.

As my wife, she subordinated her whole life to looking after me, but the strength of character that she instilled in the lives of our three children has been truly remarkable and something for which I will be eternally grateful. It has allowed them to survive in the crucible of life. They have been tested through no fault of their own and been proved worthy—a tribute, I believe, to their mother's love and perseverance. There can be no doubt that my indiscretion surely caused them untold pain, but with God's guiding hand and Claudia's loving care, they have survived.

Along with paying homage to Claudia, I also want to thank each one of my children. Although I am not completely aware of the depths of the pain they experienced in their own lives after my indiscretions, I am eternally grateful for their loyalty to our family and belief in me as a father. Their love has been proven to be unconditional.

Lastly, to the reader:

In this book I have shared my journey through various life experiences that have ultimately led me to a very special relationship with God and His Son, Jesus Christ. That journey took me from self-confidence, calling all my own shots, relying on my own talents, and essentially Edging God Out (EGO), as Ken Blanchard stated in the Foreword. This ultimately led me through the obviously painful experiences when it all came crashing down around me.

Many who read this will be able to look at the things I did as being beyond anything they would ever do. But as I shared early in the book: I would never have dreamed that I would have gotten to a place where I would do those things either. The temptations were subtle—the trap was hidden. As it says in Proverbs 14:12 (NASB), "There is a way which seems right to a man, but its end is the way of death."

Because of what happened to Adam and Eve in the Garden of Eden, I have learned that all human beings are seemingly born with an independent-from-God, self-confident nature. As set forth in Genesis 3:1-8, Satan suggested to them that God could not be trusted, and that if they ate of the forbidden fruit they would be like God and would be able to know the difference between good and evil. That fruit changed man from unity and compatibility with God, to being afraid of God and ashamed. Since the fall in Eden, the temptation for man has been to become his own god. Obviously those are huge shoes to fill.

It's no wonder that I became exhausted in my attempt of striving after success, thinking it'd bring me peace. I ended up making some terrible decisions that cost me and my loved ones dearly. But in spite of all the bad things that I was responsible for causing, by God's grace I came to a revelation that is more valuable than any possible earthly attainment, achievement, or glory.

I learned that God loved me, and I learned that I needed Him. Like the Prodigal Son, I came home in defeat, but as a result of that defeat, I found out how generous and loving my Father truly was. He wrapped His arms around me. I found a relationship that I didn't even know was possible with the God of the universe.

During the period when I was coaching at the University of Oklahoma, as I would be driving around the state recruiting or returning from a speaking engagement, I would often find myself at night on one of the state's many winding, two-lane country roads.

As I was driving along, it wasn't uncommon for an oncoming vehicle to blink its lights at me to warn me of some danger ahead on the road—whether it was a speed trap or some livestock loose on the roadway. Regardless, the blinking headlights served as a warning for me to slow down and drive carefully, knowing there was possible danger up ahead.

That is where I find myself today as I reflect on my wilderness period that followed my wrongdoings in Waco, Texas. The blinking of my headlights serves to caution you of the possibilities of danger lying up ahead.

But please realize that I am certainly not rendering advice on how to live your life. No, quite the contrary. I have often felt that advice, by its very nature, speaks down to people and, after all I have been through, I am not about to do that. My intention is merely to encourage, as I have found that tends to lift people up.

Therefore, by blinking my lights, I first want to encourage you to guard your heart. Each of us has priorities in our lives that we must protect by every means possible. As I continue to learn from my never-ending journey of God-discovery, my desire is to help people slow down and carefully consider the ramifications of any decisions that might impact these priorities.

Secondly, I implore you to seek truth regarding whatever issues you deem important: truth about your existence; truth about the future; truth about God; truth about Jesus and the Bible; truth about sin, guilt, and temptation; and truth about death and the afterlife. The best means of seeking truth I have found in my life has been by pursuing God. It wasn't until I became completely convinced of the truth of God's love and the relevance in my life of the Bible that I began to truly live.

A.W. Tozer said, "What comes into our minds when we think about God is the most important thing about us." What I learned is that my naïve view of God undoubtedly shaped the way I lived my life and affected the decisions I made. It wasn't until I was broken that I awakened to my true identity as His beloved child. That revelation allowed me to experience a greater degree of joy, hope, and peace than I ever experienced before. The work that God did in me and through me restored a feeling of purpose I had never felt before, despite being a college basketball coach for thirty-six years. My life went from performance-driven to purpose-driven, from pressure-filled to peace-abounding. God's grace freed me and changed me.

And a final reason for blinking my lights would be to encourage people who have encountered the various storms of life. There is a saying about life that either you have had something bad happen, you are in the middle of something bad happening, or you are about to have something bad happen—that no one is exempt from life-changing negative experiences.

Sometimes, these storms are the result of our own actions; other times, they are simply the result of a fallen world. Regardless of what has happened or why it has happened, I truly believe that turning the "storm" over to God is the only sure answer to any type of possible successful recovery. But this will occur only if your view of God includes a respect for His truest attributes and abilities.

With the time I have remaining here on earth, along with looking after my family, my main objective is to serve God in whatever manner and capacity He should require. In order that I see myself as God's servant, I had to learn how to forget myself. That task has taken seven decades.

My motivation is no longer to prove my worth to an unforgiving world. I no longer need somebody's approval. The only accolade I desire now is to be a "hope coach" for the downtrodden, the battered, and the broken spirited; for those people who desire to seek God for their lives.

I want to serve others now because in my darkest hour, Jesus Christ saved me, and God's grace lifted me back to life. I want to give to others what God has given to me.

You would think I would know better by now.

Right before this book was about to be officially released to the public, I was asked to speak at Grace College in Winona Lake, Indiana, where the National Christian College Athletic Association (NCCAA) was hosting its men's and women's national basketball tournament. Oddly enough, it was the first time I had been back in Indiana since appearing in front of the NCAA Infractions Committee a decade before. Now I was returning to speak about redemption, but little did I know that this return to Hoosierland would lead to an opportunity I least expected.

I had been invited to speak at the evening banquet held before the start of the tournament, but I asked the tournament director if I could also have a separate chance to address just the coaches and administrators. It was arranged, and among the attendees at my talk was the staff from the women's basketball team at Southwestern Christian University in Bethany, Oklahoma. They approached me after the talk and thanked me for what I had shared with them. Then, they purchased one of the books and asked if I would autograph it and personalize it for one of their administrators back in Oklahoma who they thought I might know, Jim Poteet. When they said the name, my ears immediately perked up, although I hadn't thought about Jim in many years.

During my first few years at the University of Oklahoma, almost forty years prior, I had butted heads with Jim on the recruiting trail. He was then serving a stint as a very successful coach at Bethany Nazarene College and had "absorbed" a couple of my Sooner players when they became disenchanted with their playing time at OU. From then on we had a friendly relationship, but I constantly kidded him not to "steal" any more of our players. From Bethany Nazarene, Jim went on to several other coaching stops, including a couple of years with Athletes in Action. Now, nearly forty years later and thirteen years after my stumble at Baylor, we were crossing paths again.

Several days after returning from the Indiana speaking engagement, Jim called me at my office at Allen Academy. We talked for several minutes about old times, and then he told me that he had read the book and felt the Holy Spirit prompting him to call me. He asked me if I ever thought I would coach at the college level again, and I told him that I really hadn't thought about it because I had been so impressed by all the new, young coaches in the profession. I did offer, however, that if I ever coached in college again, it would have to be at a small Christian school. That was all he had to hear.

As fate (or God) would have it, the Southwestern Christian University men's basketball coach had left two days prior to take a job at his alma mater, and Jim was really calling to see if I might have any interest in looking at their vacant position.

I really didn't think much about the job offer the rest of the day, as I was very happy at Allen Academy, but something told me to investigate it a little more. That evening, I casually mentioned the possibility to Claudia and was very surprised to hear the excitement in her voice. Perhaps it was because she was an OU grad or possibly because she was excited about our chance to return to college coaching again, but she definitely thought it was worth looking into. Therefore, with her encouragement, it was decided that I should make the six-hour drive from Bryan, Texas, up to Oklahoma City and give Southwestern a look.

After a day of observation and interviews, I was hooked. I really enjoyed the people that I met and, although the job would definitely be the hardest job I had ever attempted, I felt a real draw to Southwestern. Throughout my life, I had accepted most of my head coaching positions based on what I thought the school could do for me, but I now felt myself approaching the Southwestern opportunity based on what I hoped I could do for the school.

We prayed about the position for several days and on April 8, almost forty years to the day that I was announced as the OU head coach, I became the head basketball coach at Southwestern Christian University in Bethany, Oklahoma.

There was no doubt in our minds that God had orchestrated this opportunity, and we were thrilled to be obedient to His call. Claudia and I were returning to the area where my coaching career had started, as well as the area where we had met and fallen in love. Had we come full circle? I am not willing to admit all of that quite yet, but I have included this event in the book because it represents one the basic themes of the narrative—that, regardless of what happens in your life, God is never finished writing your story. I am so grateful for this opportunity and we are excited to begin our next chapter—thank you, God.

With all that I have experienced, I am now convinced that God is everything that He said He is, that His attributes detailed in the Bible are completely true. Though I felt God was a distant-being before, I now recognize and feel His presence every day in my life. Because I have seen the truth in the Bible played out through my life experiences, I also believe it implicitly as being "the inspired word of God."

As Paul Young admonished, what I have focused on has expanded and has delivered the peace I was looking for my whole life. This came through God-discovery.

Join me in forever discovering God. And together, we can all fall to grace.

SOURCE
MATERIAL

Foreword

"The majority of us cannot hear anything but ourselves . . ." from *My Utmost for His Highest* by Oswald Chambers, Discovery House Publishers, 2005, page 16.

A Note To the Reader

"You owe it to future generations to preserve the testimony . . ." from *The Purpose Driven Life* by Richard Warren, Zondervan, 2002, page 309.

Chapter 11: Imperfect Storm

"Look at his track record . . ." from *David: A Man of Passion and Destiny* by Charles Swindoll, Thomas Nelson Inc., 1997, page 182.

"When you are in a HALT . . ." is paraphrased from *Walking Wisely: Real Life Solutions for Everyday Situations* by Charles Stanley, Thomas Nelson Inc., 2002.

Chapter 12: Revelation

"Sherman McCoy wasn't the 'Master of the Universe' . . ." is paraphrased from *The Bonfire of the Vanities* by Tom Wolfe, Macmillan, 2002, page 9.

Chapter 17: Broken

"David reacted with what . . ." is paraphrased from *David: A Man of Passion and Destiny* by Charles Swindoll, Thomas Nelson Inc., 1997.

Chapter 18: Autopsy

"To be alive is to be broken . . ." from *The Ragamuffin Gospel: Good News for the Bedraggled, Beat-Up, and Burnt Out* by Brennan Manning, Doubleday Religious Publishing Group, 2008, page 86.

Chapter 21: Grace

"Grace still had, essentially, only two . . ." is paraphrased from *Captured by Grace: No One is Beyond the Reach of a Loving God* by David Jeremiah, Thomas Nelson Inc., 2006, page 33.

"Guilt, at its core, is the inability . . ." is paraphrased from *Facing Your Giants* by Max Lucado, Thorndike Press, 2008.

"Self-rejection is the greatest enemy . . ." from *Life of the Beloved: Spiritual Living in a Secular World* by Henri J.M. Nouwen, The Crossroad Publishing Company, 2002, page 33.

Chapter 23: Hope

"An allegory about holding onto a sense of personal worth despite everything . . ." from review of *The Shawshank Redemption* by Roger Ebert, September 23, 1994, http://www.rogerebert.com/reviews/the-shawshank-redemption-1994.

"He will give you a passion for something He cares about . . ." is paraphrased from *The Purpose Driven Life* by Richard Warren, Zondervan, 2002, page 96.

Chapter 24: Come Back

"The real tragedy . . ." is paraphrased from *The Purpose of Man: Designed to Worship* by A.W. Tozer, Gospel Light, 2009.

"Our second chance will most likely . . ." is paraphrased from *The Purpose Driven* Life by Richard Warren, Zondervan, 2002, page 222.

"There could be tremendous results provided . . ." is paraphrased from *The Blessings of Brokenness: Why God Allows Us to Go Through Hard Times* by Charles Stanley, Zondervan, 2010.

"No matter what has happened in our lives . . ." is paraphrased from *It's Time for Your Comeback: Don't Take a Step Back with a Setback* by Tim Storey, Harrison House, 1998.

Chapter 25: Restored

"I believe in forgiveness and giving . . ." from "Disgraced ex-Baylor coach Bliss gets shot at redemption", *USA Today*, June 23, 2010, and available at http://usatoday30.usatoday.com/sports/preps/basketball/2010-06-22-bliss-cover_N.htm

"My belief is they are a bunch of self-pious individuals . . ." from "Winning, controversy follow Bliss to high school" by Danny Robbins, *Associated Press*, May 5, 2011, and available at http://usatoday30.usatoday.com/sports/basketball/2011-05-05-3086725099_x.htm

"Endurance develops every time you reject . . ." from *The Purpose Driven Life* by Richard Warren, Zondervan, 2002, page 203. "It is vital that you stay focused . . ." from *The Purpose Driven Life* by Richard Warren, Zondervan, 2002, page 198.

Chapter 26: Service

"One morning at prayer . . ." from *The Ragamuffin Gospel: Good News for the Bedraggled, Beat-Up, and Burnt Out* by Brennan

Manning, Doubleday Religious Publishing Group, 2008, page 186.

"Apply spiritual cosmetics to make myself presentable . . ." from *The Ragamuffin Gospel: Good News for the Bedraggled, Beat-Up, and Burnt Out* by Brennan Manning, Doubleday Religious Publishing Group, 2008, page 23.

"Whatever past achievements might bring us honor . . ." from *The Ragamuffin Gospel: Good News for the Bedraggled, Beat-Up, and Burnt Out* by Brennan Manning, Doubleday Religious Publishing Group, 2008, page 55.

"The only man who has the . . ." from *The Cost of Discipleship* by Dietrich Bonhoeffer, Simon Schuster, 2012, page 51.

Chapter 27: The Calm

"Without a clear purpose . . ." from *The Purpose Driven Life* by Richard Warren, Zondervan, 2002, page 31.

"Most sweet of the Psalms of peace . . ." from *The Treasury of David: Containing an Original Exposition of the Book of Psalms, Volume 4* by Charles Haddon Spurgeon, I.K. Funk & Company, 1882, page 62.

"When we have God's ways . . ." from *The Treasury of David: Containing an Original Exposition of the Book of Psalms, Volume 4* by Charles Haddon Spurgeon, I.K. Funk & Company, 1882, page 65.

Epilogue

"What comes into our minds . . ." from *The Knowledge of the Holy* by A.W. Tozer, Harper Collins, 1978, page 1.